Hemp Astrology

Hemp Astrology

The Healing Power of the Stars

Matthew Petchinsky

Apophis Enterprises LLC

Hemp Astrology: The Healing Power of the Stars
By: Matthew Petchinsky

Introduction

The Intersection of Hemp and Astrology

Welcome to "Hemp Astrology: The Healing Power of the Stars," a comprehensive guide that delves into the fascinating interplay between hemp and astrology. In this introduction, we will explore the historical and medicinal uses of hemp, the foundational principles of astrology, and how the unique properties of hemp can be synergized with the influences of celestial bodies for holistic healing and personal growth.

Overview of Hemp's Historical and Medicinal Uses

Hemp, a versatile and ancient plant, has been cultivated for thousands of years. Its uses span a broad spectrum, from industrial applications to medicinal benefits. Historically, hemp was revered in various cultures for its durable fibers, nutritional seeds, and potent medicinal properties.

- **Historical Uses**: Hemp was one of the first plants to be spun into fiber over 10,000 years ago. Ancient civilizations, including the Chinese, Egyptians, and Greeks, utilized hemp for textiles, paper, ropes, and sails. The versatility of hemp made it an indispensable resource in ancient economies.

- **Medicinal Uses**: Medicinally, hemp has been used for centuries to treat a wide range of ailments. Traditional Chinese Medicine (TCM) documents the use of hemp seeds for digestive and anti-inflammatory purposes. In Ayurveda, hemp was used for its analgesic and anti-spasmodic properties. Modern science has identified key cannabinoids in hemp, such as CBD (cannabidiol), which have shown promise in managing pain, anxiety, epilepsy, and other health conditions.

- **Nutritional Value**: Hemp seeds are a powerhouse of nutrition, rich in essential fatty acids, proteins, vitamins, and minerals. They provide a complete source of protein, making them valuable in plant-based diets.

Introduction to Astrology and Its Significance

Astrology, the study of celestial bodies' movements and their influence on human affairs and natural phenomena, has been practiced for millennia. It offers a framework for understanding ourselves and the universe, emphasizing the interconnectedness of all things.

- **Foundations of Astrology**: At its core, astrology is based on the belief that the positions and movements of celestial bodies—such as planets, stars, and the Moon—affect human lives and events on Earth. This ancient practice is divided into various systems and traditions, including Western astrology, Vedic astrology, and Chinese astrology, each with its own unique methods and interpretations.
- **The Zodiac Signs**: The zodiac is a belt of the heavens divided into twelve equal parts, each named after the constellation that appears in that section. These zodiac signs—Aries, Taurus, Gemini, Cancer, Leo, Virgo, Libra, Scorpio, Sagittarius, Capricorn, Aquarius, and Pisces—are central to Western astrology. Each sign is associated with specific traits, behaviors, and tendencies, providing insights into personality and potential life paths.
- **Astrological Houses and Aspects**: Astrology also considers the twelve houses, each representing different areas of life, from personal identity and wealth to relationships and spirituality. Aspects, the angles formed between planets, further refine astrological readings, highlighting areas of harmony, tension, and potential growth.
- **The Role of the Sun, Moon, and Rising Signs**: In a natal chart, the Sun sign represents core identity, the Moon sign reflects emotional nature, and the rising sign (or ascendant) indicates how

one presents themselves to the world. Together, these elements create a holistic picture of an individual's astrological makeup.

The Synergy Between Hemp's Healing Properties and the Influences of Celestial Bodies

The concept of integrating hemp and astrology may seem novel, but both share a common goal: enhancing well-being and fostering a deeper connection with the universe.

- **Hemp's Healing Properties**: Hemp's medicinal benefits can be aligned with astrological insights to support holistic health. For instance, hemp's calming effects can help balance the emotional turbulence often associated with certain lunar phases or planetary transits.
- **Astrological Influences**: Each zodiac sign and celestial event has specific energies and attributes that influence our lives. By understanding these influences, we can use hemp to complement and enhance these energies. For example, during a Full Moon, known for heightened emotions and illumination, hemp can provide grounding and clarity.
- **Personal Growth and Transformation**: Combining hemp and astrology creates a powerful tool for personal growth. Whether it's using hemp-infused meditation to align with planetary transits or incorporating hemp-based rituals during significant astrological events, this integration allows for a more profound and intentional approach to self-care and spiritual practice.

In this book, you will embark on a journey that bridges ancient wisdom with modern practices, exploring how hemp and astrology can work together to enhance your life. From understanding the Moon's phases and their impact on emotions to harnessing the power of planetary alignments with hemp rituals, "Hemp Astrology: The Healing Power of the Stars" offers practical insights and transformative practices for a holistic approach to well-being. Let's begin this enlightening exploration into the cosmic and earthly realms, where hemp and astrology meet to create harmony and healing.

Chapter 1: The Basics of Hemp
History and Origins of Hemp

Hemp, one of the earliest known cultivated plants, has a rich and diverse history that spans over 10,000 years. Its origins can be traced back to ancient civilizations where it was revered for its versatility and strength.

- **Ancient Beginnings**: Archaeological evidence suggests that hemp was first cultivated in ancient China around 8,000 BCE. It was primarily grown for its fibers, which were used to make ropes, textiles, and paper. The ancient Chinese recognized the plant's medicinal properties early on, using hemp seeds and oils for a variety of treatments.
- **Spread to Other Cultures**: From China, hemp cultivation spread to other parts of Asia, including India and the Middle East. In India, it became a key ingredient in Ayurvedic medicine, valued for its analgesic and anti-inflammatory properties. The Scythians, an ancient group of nomadic warriors, introduced hemp to Europe around 2,000 BCE, where it was used to make clothing, sails, and ropes.
- **Hemp in Europe**: By the Middle Ages, hemp was a staple crop across Europe. It was extensively used in the production of textiles, ropes for ships, and as a medicinal plant. The famous Italian explorer, Marco Polo, documented the use of hemp in various cultures he encountered on his travels, highlighting its widespread acceptance and utility.
- **Colonial America**: Hemp played a crucial role in the early history of America. The first American settlers brought hemp seeds with them and were mandated by law to grow hemp as a vital crop for the colony's survival. Hemp was used for making ropes, sails, and

clothing, critical to the maritime economy. Even the first drafts of the Declaration of Independence were written on hemp paper.

- **20th Century Decline**: The 20th century saw a decline in hemp cultivation due to political and economic factors. The Marihuana Tax Act of 1937 in the United States heavily taxed the production of hemp, conflating it with its psychoactive cousin, marijuana. This led to a significant reduction in hemp farming. Later, the Controlled Substances Act of 1970 classified all cannabis, including hemp, as a Schedule I drug, further stifling its cultivation.
- **Modern Revival**: The late 20th and early 21st centuries have seen a resurgence of interest in hemp, driven by its potential for sustainable agriculture and its medicinal properties. Legislation such as the 2018 Farm Bill in the United States has reclassified hemp, making it legal to grow and process under certain conditions, sparking a new era of hemp innovation.

Chemical Composition and Key Cannabinoids

Understanding the chemical composition of hemp is essential to appreciate its wide range of uses and benefits. Hemp contains over 400 different compounds, including cannabinoids, terpenes, flavonoids, and essential fatty acids.

- **Cannabinoids**: Cannabinoids are the most studied and well-known compounds in hemp. The two primary cannabinoids found in hemp are:
    - **CBD (Cannabidiol)**: Unlike THC, CBD is non-psychoactive, meaning it doesn't produce a "high." It is renowned for its therapeutic benefits, including pain relief, anti-inflammatory properties, anxiety reduction, and seizure management. CBD interacts with the body's endocannabinoid system (ECS) to promote homeostasis.
    - **THC (Tetrahydrocannabinol)**: Hemp contains only trace amounts of THC (less than 0.3%), which is not enough

to produce psychoactive effects. This low THC content differentiates hemp from marijuana.

- **Other Cannabinoids**: Hemp also contains other cannabinoids like CBG (Cannabigerol), CBC (Cannabichromene), and CBN (Cannabinol), each contributing to its therapeutic potential.
  - ◦ **CBG**: Often referred to as the "mother of all cannabinoids," CBG is a precursor to other cannabinoids. It shows promise in reducing inflammation, pain, and nausea.
  - ◦ **CBC**: Known for its potential anti-depressant, anti-inflammatory, and anti-cancer properties.
  - ◦ **CBN**: Primarily found in aged cannabis, CBN is believed to have sedative effects and is often used for sleep disorders.
- **Terpenes and Flavonoids**: These compounds are responsible for the plant's aroma and flavor, and they also contribute to its therapeutic effects. Terpenes like myrcene, limonene, and pinene have various health benefits, including anti-inflammatory and anti-anxiety effects. Flavonoids, such as quercetin and kaempferol, have antioxidant and anti-inflammatory properties.
- **Essential Fatty Acids**: Hemp seeds are rich in omega-3 and omega-6 fatty acids, which are crucial for heart health, brain function, and reducing inflammation.

Different Uses of Hemp: Industrial, Medicinal, and Recreational
Hemp's versatility makes it valuable across multiple industries, from textiles and construction to medicine and wellness.

- **Industrial Uses**: Hemp's strong fibers have been utilized in various industrial applications for centuries.
  - ◦ **Textiles**: Hemp fibers are used to make durable fabrics for clothing, shoes, and accessories. Hemp textiles are breathable, resistant to mold and UV light, and environmentally friendly.

- **Paper**: Hemp paper is a sustainable alternative to wood pulp paper, requiring fewer chemicals and producing more paper per acre of hemp than trees.
- **Building Materials**: Hempcrete, a mixture of hemp hurds and lime, is a sustainable building material that is lightweight, insulating, and carbon-negative. It is used for constructing energy-efficient buildings.
- **Bioplastics**: Hemp can be used to produce biodegradable plastics, reducing reliance on petroleum-based plastics and mitigating environmental pollution.

- **Medicinal Uses**: The therapeutic potential of hemp is being increasingly recognized in modern medicine.
  - **Pain Relief**: Hemp-derived CBD is widely used for its analgesic properties, helping to alleviate chronic pain, arthritis, and neuropathic pain.
  - **Anti-Inflammatory**: Hemp's anti-inflammatory effects make it beneficial for treating conditions like rheumatoid arthritis, inflammatory bowel disease, and skin disorders such as eczema and psoriasis.
  - **Anxiety and Depression**: CBD has shown promise in reducing symptoms of anxiety and depression, offering a natural alternative to pharmaceutical treatments.
  - **Epilepsy and Seizure Disorders**: CBD has been approved by the FDA for treating certain types of epilepsy, such as Dravet syndrome and Lennox-Gastaut syndrome.
  - **Neuroprotection**: Emerging research suggests that CBD may have neuroprotective properties, potentially benefiting conditions like Alzheimer's disease, Parkinson's disease, and multiple sclerosis.

- **Recreational Uses**: While hemp itself is not psychoactive, its derivative, CBD, is used recreationally for its calming and relaxing effects.

- **Wellness Products**: CBD oils, tinctures, and edibles are popular for promoting relaxation and general well-being. These products are used to enhance mood, improve sleep quality, and reduce stress.
- **Skincare**: Hemp-derived CBD is incorporated into skincare products for its anti-inflammatory and antioxidant properties, helping to soothe irritated skin and promote a healthy complexion.

In this chapter, we have explored the rich history and diverse applications of hemp, highlighting its importance across various industries. Understanding the basics of hemp provides a solid foundation for appreciating its potential when combined with the ancient wisdom of astrology. As we journey further into this book, we will discover how the healing properties of hemp can be synergized with the influences of celestial bodies to enhance our well-being and foster a deeper connection with the universe.

Check out my Virtual dispensary for all your hemp needs: https://shift.store/sg1fan23477/retail

Chapter 2: Introduction to Astrology

The Fundamentals of Astrology: Zodiac Signs, Houses, and Aspects

Astrology is an ancient practice that explores the relationship between celestial bodies and human experiences. It is based on the belief that the positions and movements of the stars and planets influence our lives, personalities, and behaviors. To understand astrology, one must become familiar with its core components: zodiac signs, houses, and aspects.

- **Zodiac Signs**: The zodiac is a belt of the heavens divided into twelve equal parts, each associated with a specific constellation. These twelve divisions are known as zodiac signs, each governing distinct personality traits, behaviors, and life paths. The signs are:
  1. **Aries (March 21 - April 19)**: Courageous, dynamic, and energetic.
  2. **Taurus (April 20 - May 20)**: Reliable, patient, and practical.
  3. **Gemini (May 21 - June 20)**: Adaptable, curious, and communicative.
  4. **Cancer (June 21 - July 22)**: Nurturing, intuitive, and protective.

5. **Leo (July 23 - August 22)**: Confident, generous, and charismatic.
6. **Virgo (August 23 - September 22)**: Analytical, meticulous, and dependable.
7. **Libra (September 23 - October 22)**: Diplomatic, artistic, and sociable.
8. **Scorpio (October 23 - November 21)**: Intense, passionate, and resourceful.
9. **Sagittarius (November 22 - December 21)**: Adventurous, optimistic, and philosophical.
10. **Capricorn (December 22 - January 19)**: Ambitious, disciplined, and practical.
11. **Aquarius (January 20 - February 18)**: Innovative, humanitarian, and independent.
12. **Pisces (February 19 - March 20)**: Compassionate, imaginative, and intuitive.

- **Astrological Houses**: The astrological chart is divided into twelve houses, each representing different areas of life. The houses are as follows:
  1. **First House (House of Self)**: Personal identity, appearance, and first impressions.
  2. **Second House (House of Value)**: Finances, possessions, and self-worth.
  3. **Third House (House of Communication)**: Communication, siblings, and local travel.
  4. **Fourth House (House of Home)**: Home, family, and foundations.
  5. **Fifth House (House of Pleasure)**: Creativity, romance, and children.
  6. **Sixth House (House of Health)**: Health, work, and daily routines.
  7. **Seventh House (House of Partnerships)**: Relationships, marriage, and partnerships.

8. **Eighth House (House of Transformation)**: Transformation, sex, and shared resources.

9. **Ninth House (House of Philosophy)**: Higher education, travel, and philosophy.

10. **Tenth House (House of Social Status)**: Career, reputation, and public roles.

11. **Eleventh House (House of Friendships)**: Friendships, groups, and aspirations.

12. **Twelfth House (House of Subconscious)**: Subconscious, spirituality, and hidden matters.

- **Aspects**: Aspects are the angles formed between planets on the astrological chart, influencing how they interact. Major aspects include:

    1. **Conjunction (0°)**: Planets are close together, combining their energies.

    2. **Sextile (60°)**: Planets form a supportive relationship, encouraging cooperation.

    3. **Square (90°)**: Planets are in conflict, creating tension and challenges.

    4. **Trine (120°)**: Planets flow harmoniously, fostering ease and opportunity.

    5. **Opposition (180°)**: Planets are directly opposite, indicating balance or conflict.

The Twelve Zodiac Signs and Their Characteristics

Each zodiac sign embodies distinct characteristics, shaping personality traits, behaviors, and preferences. Here is an overview of the twelve zodiac signs and their key attributes:

1. **Aries (March 21 - April 19)**
    - **Element**: Fire
    - **Ruling Planet**: Mars

- **Key Traits**: Courageous, energetic, assertive, and adventurous. Aries individuals are natural leaders who thrive on challenges and excitement. They are often pioneers and trailblazers.

2. **Taurus (April 20 - May 20)**
   - **Element**: Earth
   - **Ruling Planet**: Venus
   - **Key Traits**: Reliable, patient, practical, and determined. Taurus individuals value stability, comfort, and material security. They are known for their strong work ethic and love of beauty and luxury.

3. **Gemini (May 21 - June 20)**
   - **Element**: Air
   - **Ruling Planet**: Mercury
   - **Key Traits**: Adaptable, curious, communicative, and witty. Gemini individuals are versatile and enjoy intellectual stimulation. They thrive in social settings and excel at communication.

4. **Cancer (June 21 - July 22)**
   - **Element**: Water
   - **Ruling Planet**: Moon
   - **Key Traits**: Nurturing, intuitive, protective, and empathetic. Cancer individuals are deeply connected to their emotions and the well-being of others. They are often seen as the caregivers and protectors of their loved ones.

5. **Leo (July 23 - August 22)**
   - **Element**: Fire
   - **Ruling Planet**: Sun
   - **Key Traits**: Confident, generous, charismatic, and creative. Leo individuals have a natural flair for leadership and enjoy being in the spotlight. They are warm-hearted and have a strong sense of pride.

6. **Virgo (August 23 - September 22)**

- ○ **Element**: Earth
- ○ **Ruling Planet**: Mercury
- ○ **Key Traits**: Analytical, meticulous, dependable, and practical. Virgo individuals are detail-oriented and strive for perfection. They are often seen as reliable and hardworking, with a strong sense of duty.

7. **Libra (September 23 - October 22)**
   - ○ **Element**: Air
   - ○ **Ruling Planet**: Venus
   - ○ **Key Traits**: Diplomatic, artistic, sociable, and fair-minded. Libra individuals seek balance and harmony in all aspects of life. They have a strong sense of justice and are often drawn to artistic and aesthetic pursuits.

8. **Scorpio (October 23 - November 21)**
   - ○ **Element**: Water
   - ○ **Ruling Planet**: Pluto
   - ○ **Key Traits**: Intense, passionate, resourceful, and determined. Scorpio individuals are known for their depth of emotion and their transformative nature. They are often driven by a desire for power and control.

9. **Sagittarius (November 22 - December 21)**
   - ○ **Element**: Fire
   - ○ **Ruling Planet**: Jupiter
   - ○ **Key Traits**: Adventurous, optimistic, philosophical, and independent. Sagittarius individuals have a love for exploration and learning. They are known for their positive outlook on life and their quest for truth and knowledge.

10. **Capricorn (December 22 - January 19)**

- **Element**: Earth
- **Ruling Planet**: Saturn

- **Key Traits**: Ambitious, disciplined, practical, and responsible. Capricorn individuals are focused on achieving their goals and are known for their perseverance and strong sense of responsibility.

1. **Aquarius (January 20 - February 18)**

- **Element**: Air
- **Ruling Planet**: Uranus
- **Key Traits**: Innovative, humanitarian, independent, and intellectual. Aquarius individuals are often seen as visionaries and are driven by a desire to improve the world. They value their independence and unique perspectives.

1. **Pisces (February 19 - March 20)**

- **Element**: Water
- **Ruling Planet**: Neptune
- **Key Traits**: Compassionate, imaginative, intuitive, and empathetic. Pisces individuals are deeply connected to their emotions and the spiritual realm. They are known for their artistic talents and their ability to understand others' feelings.

The Role of the Sun, Moon, and Rising Signs

In astrology, the Sun, Moon, and rising signs are the three most significant components of an individual's natal chart, each representing different aspects of the self.

- **Sun Sign**: The Sun sign is determined by the position of the Sun at the time of one's birth and represents the core of one's personality and identity. It reflects one's ego, vitality, and basic character. The Sun sign is often what people refer to when they say, "I am a Taurus" or "I am a Leo."

- **Moon Sign**: The Moon sign is determined by the position of the Moon at the time of birth and represents one's emotional nature and inner self. It governs how one feels, reacts, and processes emotions. The Moon sign reveals one's deepest needs and instinctual responses.
- **Rising Sign (Ascendant)**: The rising sign, or ascendant, is the zodiac sign that was rising on the eastern horizon at the time of birth. It represents one's outward behavior, appearance, and the first impression one makes on others. The rising sign is like a mask that one wears when interacting with the world, influencing how others perceive them.

Together, the Sun, Moon, and rising signs create a holistic picture of an individual's astrological makeup, providing insights into their core identity, emotional responses, and outward demeanor.

In this chapter, we have explored the fundamental principles of astrology, including the zodiac signs, houses, and aspects, as well as the roles of the Sun, Moon, and rising signs. Understanding these basics provides a foundation for delving deeper into the intricate and multi-faceted world of astrology. As we continue our journey through this book, we will discover how these astrological elements interact with the healing properties of hemp to enhance our well-being and foster a deeper connection with the universe.

Check out my Virtual dispensary for all your hemp needs: https://shift.store/sg1fan23477/retail

Chapter 3: The Moon and Its Phases
The Eight Phases of the Moon
The Moon's phases are a result of its orbit around the Earth, changing the portion of the Moon that is illuminated by the Sun. There are eight primary phases, each with unique characteristics and influences.

1. **New Moon**: The Moon is positioned between the Earth and the Sun, making it invisible from Earth. This phase represents new beginnings, setting intentions, and fresh starts.
2. **Waxing Crescent**: A sliver of the Moon becomes visible. This phase symbolizes growth, potential, and the nurturing of new ideas and projects.
3. **First Quarter**: Half of the Moon is illuminated. This phase is about taking action, making decisions, and overcoming obstacles.
4. **Waxing Gibbous**: More than half of the Moon is visible, but it is not yet full. This phase signifies refinement, preparation, and continued progress.
5. **Full Moon**: The entire face of the Moon is illuminated. This phase represents culmination, illumination, and heightened emotions.
6. **Waning Gibbous**: The Moon starts to decrease in illumination. This phase is about gratitude, introspection, and releasing what no longer serves us.
7. **Last Quarter**: Again, half of the Moon is visible. This phase signifies letting go, forgiveness, and reevaluation.
8. **Waning Crescent**: A small sliver of the Moon is visible before it disappears completely. This phase represents rest, reflection, and preparing for the new cycle.

How the Moon's Phases Influence Emotions and Behavior
The Moon has a profound effect on our emotions and behavior, influencing our inner world and outward actions. Each phase brings its

own energy, which can be harnessed to enhance personal growth and well-being.

1. **New Moon**: This phase is ideal for introspection and setting intentions. The energy is quiet and reflective, encouraging us to plant seeds for the future. Emotionally, we may feel a sense of renewal and a desire to start fresh.

2. **Waxing Crescent**: As the Moon begins to grow, so does our motivation and energy. This phase encourages us to take the first steps toward our goals. Emotionally, we might feel optimistic and full of potential.

3. **First Quarter**: This phase can bring challenges and the need for decisive action. The energy is assertive and dynamic, pushing us to confront obstacles. Emotionally, we may feel a sense of urgency and determination.

4. **Waxing Gibbous**: The focus during this phase is on refinement and preparation. We are encouraged to perfect our plans and continue working diligently. Emotionally, we might feel anticipation and a drive to complete tasks.

5. **Full Moon**: Emotions run high during the Full Moon, as everything is brought to light. This is a time of celebration, manifestation, and emotional release. We may experience heightened sensitivity and clarity.

6. **Waning Gibbous**: As the Moon begins to wane, the energy shifts to gratitude and introspection. This phase encourages us to appreciate what we have accomplished and to let go of what is no longer needed. Emotionally, we may feel reflective and grateful.

7. **Last Quarter**: This phase is about releasing and letting go. The energy supports forgiveness and making space for new growth. Emotionally, we may feel a need to clean house, both physically and emotionally.

8. **Waning Crescent**: The final phase is a time of rest and preparation. The energy is quiet and introspective, encouraging us to

reflect on the past cycle and prepare for the new one. Emotionally, we may feel a need for solitude and contemplation.

Using Hemp to Align with the Moon's Energy

Hemp, with its versatile properties, can be used to enhance and align with the Moon's phases. By incorporating hemp into our routines, we can amplify the benefits of each phase and support our emotional and physical well-being.

1. **New Moon**: Use hemp products that promote relaxation and introspection, such as CBD oils or tinctures. These can help calm the mind and create a peaceful environment for setting intentions. Meditative practices with hemp can deepen your connection to your inner self.

2. **Waxing Crescent**: Hemp products that boost energy and focus, such as hemp protein powders or CBD-infused snacks, can support the growth and nurturing of new ideas. Incorporate these into your diet to maintain motivation and clarity.

3. **First Quarter**: During this action-oriented phase, use hemp products that enhance physical stamina and mental alertness. CBD topicals can soothe any physical stress from increased activity, while CBD capsules can help maintain focus and determination.

4. **Waxing Gibbous**: As you refine and prepare, use hemp products that support mental clarity and relaxation. Hemp teas and CBD-infused beverages can help keep you balanced and focused on perfecting your plans.

5. **Full Moon**: Enhance your Full Moon rituals with hemp products that promote emotional release and celebration. CBD bath bombs or hemp candles can create a serene atmosphere for meditation and manifestation. Use hemp-infused lotions for a calming self-care routine.

6. **Waning Gibbous**: During this phase of gratitude and introspection, use hemp products that support reflection and relaxation. CBD gummies or hemp-infused chocolate can be a delightful way to unwind and appreciate your accomplishments.

7. **Last Quarter**: As you release and let go, incorporate hemp products that promote detoxification and renewal. Hemp seed oil can be used in salads or smoothies to support physical cleansing, while CBD oils can aid in emotional release.

8. **Waning Crescent**: In this final phase of rest and preparation, use hemp products that promote deep relaxation and sleep. CBD sleep aids, such as capsules or gummies, can ensure restorative rest, preparing you for the new cycle.

In this chapter, we have explored the eight phases of the Moon, how they influence our emotions and behavior, and how hemp can be used to align with the Moon's energy. By understanding the natural rhythms of the Moon and incorporating hemp into our routines, we can enhance our well-being and harness the power of these celestial cycles. As we continue our journey through this book, we will discover even more ways to integrate hemp and astrology for holistic healing and personal growth.

Check out my Virtual dispensary for all your hemp needs: https://shift.store/sg1fan23477/retail

Chapter 4: New Moon Rituals with Hemp
Setting Intentions During the New Moon

The New Moon represents a time of new beginnings, making it an ideal phase for setting intentions. During this phase, the Moon is not visible from Earth, symbolizing a blank slate upon which to project our goals and aspirations. Setting intentions during the New Moon helps focus your energy and manifest your desires.

- **Creating a Sacred Space**: Before setting your intentions, create a sacred space where you can feel calm and centered. This space should be free from distractions and filled with items that inspire you, such as crystals, candles, and plants. Incorporate hemp items, such as a hemp yoga mat or a hemp-infused candle, to enhance the atmosphere.
- **Journaling Your Intentions**: Write down your intentions in a journal. Be specific about what you want to achieve and how you want to feel. Use affirmative language and write as if your intentions have already been manifested. For example, instead of saying, "I want to be healthy," say, "I am healthy and vibrant."
- **Visualizing Your Goals**: Visualization is a powerful tool for manifesting intentions. Close your eyes and imagine your life after your intentions have been realized. Feel the emotions associated with your success and immerse yourself in the experience. Visualization helps to solidify your intentions in your subconscious mind.
- **Hemp-Infused Affirmations**: Incorporate hemp-based products such as CBD oil or hemp tea during your intention-setting ritual. These can help calm your mind and body, making it easier to

focus on your intentions. As you use these products, repeat affirmations that align with your goals, reinforcing your commitment to your intentions.

Hemp-Infused Meditation and Rituals

Meditation is a powerful practice that can help you align with the New Moon's energy. By incorporating hemp into your meditation rituals, you can deepen your practice and enhance the manifestation of your intentions.

- **CBD Meditation Oils**: Using CBD-infused oils can enhance relaxation and focus during meditation. Apply a few drops of CBD oil to your temples or wrists before starting your meditation. This can help calm your mind and reduce any anxiety, allowing you to fully immerse yourself in the practice.
- **Hemp Candles and Incense**: Light a hemp-infused candle or incense to create a serene environment. The gentle scent of hemp can help soothe your senses and create a calming atmosphere, conducive to meditation and reflection.
- **Guided Meditation with Hemp**: Follow a guided meditation that incorporates hemp. There are many online resources and apps that offer guided meditations focused on intention setting and manifesting during the New Moon. These meditations often include visualization techniques and affirmations to help you connect with your goals.
- **Hemp-Infused Herbal Tea**: Drinking hemp-infused herbal tea before or after your meditation can enhance relaxation and clarity. Choose a blend that includes calming herbs such as chamomile or lavender, along with hemp, to support a peaceful state of mind.
- **Crystals and Hemp**: Incorporate crystals known for their manifestation properties, such as citrine or clear quartz, into your meditation space. Use hemp string to create a crystal grid or to

wrap the crystals, enhancing their energy and connection to your intentions.

- **Breathwork and Hemp**: Combine breathwork practices with the use of hemp products. Deep, intentional breathing can help center your mind and body, while CBD or hemp-infused products can support relaxation and focus. Practice deep breathing exercises to enhance your meditation and intention-setting rituals.

In this chapter, we have explored the importance of setting intentions during the New Moon, the benefits of hemp-infused meditation and rituals. By integrating hemp into your New Moon rituals, you can enhance your ability to manifest your desires and achieve personal growth. As we continue our journey through this book, we will uncover more ways to harness the synergy between hemp and astrology for holistic healing and well-being.

Check out my Virtual dispensary for all your hemp needs: https://shift.store/sg1fan23477/retail

Chapter 5: Waxing Crescent and Waxing Gibbous Phases Embracing Growth and Manifestation

The Waxing Crescent and Waxing Gibbous phases of the Moon are periods of growth, development, and manifestation. These phases encourage us to take the initial steps toward our goals and continue building momentum as we refine and prepare for their realization.

- **Waxing Crescent Phase**: This phase occurs just after the New Moon, as a small sliver of the Moon becomes visible. It symbolizes the sprouting of new ideas and the nurturing of intentions set during the New Moon. This is a time of optimism, motivation, and forward movement.

- **Embracing Growth**: The Waxing Crescent phase invites us to embrace growth by taking actionable steps toward our goals. It's about nurturing the seeds of intention planted during the New Moon and giving them the care and attention they need to thrive. This phase is ideal for starting new projects, learning new skills, and making plans.

- **Waxing Gibbous Phase**: As the Moon continues to grow, it enters the Waxing Gibbous phase, where more than half of it is illuminated. This phase represents refinement, preparation, and the buildup to the Full Moon. It's a time to focus on details, make adjustments, and ensure everything is on track.

- **Manifestation**: The Waxing Gibbous phase is about manifesting our intentions by diligently working toward our goals. It encourages us to stay committed, overcome obstacles, and fine-tune our plans. This phase is perfect for putting in the necessary effort and dedication to see our intentions come to fruition.

Hemp Products for Focus and Motivation

Hemp products can be incredibly beneficial during the Waxing Crescent and Waxing Gibbous phases by providing the focus and motivation needed to pursue our goals. Here are some hemp products that can support growth and manifestation:

- **CBD Oil**: CBD oil is known for its calming and focusing effects. It can help reduce anxiety and stress, allowing you to concentrate on your tasks and stay motivated. Take a few drops of CBD oil in the morning or before starting a project to enhance focus and clarity.
- **Hemp Protein Powder**: Hemp protein powder is an excellent source of energy and nutrition. It provides a balanced blend of protein, essential fatty acids, and fiber, making it a great addition to smoothies or snacks. Consuming hemp protein can boost your energy levels and sustain you through periods of intense work.
- **Hemp-Infused Energy Bars**: Hemp-infused energy bars are convenient and nutritious snacks that can keep you fueled and focused throughout the day. Look for bars that include other superfoods like chia seeds, nuts, and dried fruits for added benefits.
- **CBD Capsules**: CBD capsules offer a convenient way to incorporate CBD into your daily routine. They can help maintain steady levels of CBD in your system, supporting ongoing focus and motivation. Take them with your morning vitamins or before a challenging task.
- **Hemp Tea**: Hemp tea blends can provide a calming and clarifying effect, perfect for moments when you need to focus. Choose blends that include other herbs like ginseng or peppermint for added mental stimulation and energy.

- **Topical CBD Products**: Topical CBD products like balms and creams can help alleviate physical discomfort and tension, allowing you to stay focused on your tasks. Apply them to areas of tension, such as the neck and shoulders, to relieve stress and improve your ability to concentrate.

Practical Applications and Exercises

To harness the energy of the Waxing Crescent and Waxing Gibbous phases, it's important to incorporate practical applications and exercises into your routine. Here are some effective ways to align with these phases:

- **Daily Affirmations**: Start each day with positive affirmations that reinforce your goals and intentions. Write down affirmations related to growth and manifestation, such as "I am capable of achieving my goals" or "I am motivated and focused on my path."
- **Goal Setting and Planning**: Use this time to set clear, actionable goals. Break down your larger intentions into smaller, manageable tasks. Create a plan or a to-do list to keep track of your progress and stay organized.
- **Visualization Exercises**: Spend a few minutes each day visualizing your goals as already achieved. Imagine the steps you need to take and how you will feel once you reach your objectives. Visualization helps solidify your intentions and keeps you motivated.
- **Meditation with Hemp**: Incorporate hemp products into your meditation practice to enhance focus and relaxation. Use CBD oil or drink hemp tea before meditating. Focus on your breath and visualize your intentions growing and manifesting.
- **Physical Activity**: Engage in physical activities that promote energy and motivation, such as yoga, jogging, or dancing. Physical exercise not only boosts your energy levels but also helps clear your mind and improve focus.

- **Creative Projects**: The Waxing Crescent phase is an excellent time to start creative projects. Whether it's writing, painting, or crafting, allow yourself to explore new ideas and express your creativity. Use hemp products like CBD-infused art supplies or hemp paper for an added touch.
- **Reflection and Refinement**: During the Waxing Gibbous phase, take time to reflect on your progress. Review your goals and make any necessary adjustments. Refine your plans and ensure that everything is aligned with your intentions.
- **Journaling**: Keep a journal to document your thoughts, progress, and any insights you gain during these phases. Writing down your experiences can help clarify your intentions and keep you motivated.
- **Accountability Partner**: Partner with someone who shares similar goals. Check in with each other regularly to share progress, offer support, and stay accountable.

In this chapter, we have explored the importance of the Waxing Crescent and Waxing Gibbous phases, focusing on growth and manifestation. We have discussed how hemp products can support focus and motivation and provided practical applications and exercises to help you align with these phases. By embracing the energy of the Waxing Moon and incorporating hemp into your routine, you can enhance your ability to manifest your intentions and achieve your goals. As we continue our journey through this book, we will uncover more ways to harness the synergy between hemp and astrology for holistic healing and personal growth.

Check out my Virtual dispensary for all your hemp needs: https://shift.store/sg1fan23477/retail

Chapter 6: Full Moon Power
The Significance of the Full Moon in Astrology
The Full Moon is one of the most potent and mystical phases of the lunar cycle. In astrology, the Full Moon occurs when the Sun and Moon are in opposition, meaning they are directly across from each other in the sky. This alignment creates a sense of balance and heightened energy, bringing emotions, desires, and intentions to the forefront.

- **Symbolism**: The Full Moon symbolizes completion, illumination, and fulfillment. It is a time when the seeds planted during the New Moon reach their peak, and intentions come to fruition. The Full Moon's bright light shines on hidden aspects of our lives, revealing truths and bringing clarity.
- **Emotional Intensity**: The Full Moon is known to amplify emotions, making it a period of heightened sensitivity and intensity. This can lead to breakthroughs, emotional releases, and profound insights. It is an ideal time for reflection, celebration, and letting go of what no longer serves us.
- **Astrological Impact**: Each Full Moon occurs in a specific zodiac sign, influencing its energy and themes. For example, a Full Moon in Aries may bring themes of courage and action, while a Full Moon in Pisces may focus on intuition and spirituality. Understanding the sign in which the Full Moon occurs can provide deeper insights into its potential impact on your life.

Harnessing the Full Moon's Energy with Hemp
The Full Moon's powerful energy can be harnessed and amplified with the use of hemp. Incorporating hemp into your Full Moon rituals can enhance your ability to connect with this lunar phase and maximize its benefits.

- **CBD for Emotional Balance**: The Full Moon's intense energy can sometimes lead to emotional overwhelm. CBD oil can help balance emotions and promote a sense of calm. Take a few drops of CBD oil under your tongue or add it to a beverage to help manage heightened emotions and maintain clarity.
- **Hemp Candles for Atmosphere**: Create a serene and magical atmosphere with hemp-infused candles. The gentle scent of hemp can soothe your senses and help you focus on your rituals. Light hemp candles during your Full Moon practices to enhance the ambiance and energy of your space.
- **Hemp Tea for Relaxation**: Drinking hemp-infused herbal tea can help you relax and center your mind during the Full Moon. Choose a blend that includes calming herbs such as chamomile, lavender, and passionflower, combined with hemp, to promote relaxation and mindfulness.
- **CBD Bath Bombs for Cleansing**: A ritual bath with a CBD-infused bath bomb can be a powerful way to cleanse and rejuvenate your body and spirit. The Full Moon is a perfect time for cleansing rituals, and a CBD bath can help you release negative energy, relax your muscles, and refresh your mind.
- **Hemp Journals for Reflection**: Use a hemp journal to document your thoughts, insights, and experiences during the Full Moon. Writing can help you process emotions and gain clarity. Reflect on your journey since the last New Moon and set intentions for the next lunar cycle.

Rituals, Practices, and Real-Life Examples

Engaging in rituals and practices during the Full Moon can help you harness its energy for personal growth and transformation. Here are some detailed rituals and practices, along with real-life examples of their benefits:

- **Full Moon Meditation**: Meditation during the Full Moon can help you connect with its energy and gain insights. Sit in a comfortable position, light a hemp candle, and focus on your breath. Visualize the Full Moon's light surrounding you, illuminating your mind and spirit. Allow any emotions or thoughts to surface without judgment. This practice can bring clarity and emotional release.

- **Moonlight Ritual**: Spend time outside under the Full Moon's light. Stand barefoot on the ground, close your eyes, and breathe deeply. Feel the Moon's energy flowing through you, cleansing and recharging your spirit. You can also place crystals or other sacred objects under the Moonlight to cleanse and charge them with lunar energy.

- **Release and Let Go**: The Full Moon is an ideal time to release what no longer serves you. Write down any negative thoughts, habits, or situations you want to let go of on a piece of paper. Use a hemp candle to safely burn the paper, visualizing the release of these burdens from your life. As the paper turns to ash, feel a sense of liberation and renewal.

- **Gratitude Ritual**: Take time to express gratitude for the blessings in your life. Use a hemp journal to write down things you are grateful for. Reflect on the progress you have made since the New Moon and acknowledge your achievements. This practice can elevate your mood and attract more positive energy.

- **Group Full Moon Ritual**: Gather with friends or a like-minded community to perform a Full Moon ritual together. Create a sacred circle, light hemp candles, and share your intentions and experiences. Group rituals can amplify the Full Moon's energy and provide a sense of connection and support.

- **Crystal Healing**: Use crystals that resonate with the Full Moon's energy, such as moonstone, selenite, and clear quartz. Hold the crystals or place them on your body during meditation to enhance your connection with the lunar energy. You can also create a crystal grid using hemp string to amplify their healing properties.

In this chapter, we have explored the significance of the Full Moon in astrology, the benefits of harnessing its energy with hemp, and various rituals and practices to enhance your connection with this powerful lunar phase. By incorporating hemp into your Full Moon rituals, you can amplify the Moon's energy, achieve emotional balance, and manifest your intentions. As we continue our journey through this book, we will discover more ways to integrate hemp and astrology for holistic healing and personal growth.

Check out my Virtual dispensary for all your hemp needs: https://shift.store/sg1fan23477/retail

Chapter 7: Waning Phases and Reflection
The Waning Gibbous and Waning Crescent Phases

As the Full Moon begins to wane, it enters a period of reflection, release, and preparation for the next lunar cycle. The waning phases are times of introspection and letting go of what no longer serves us.

- **Waning Gibbous Phase**: Following the Full Moon, the Waning Gibbous phase begins. During this phase, the Moon starts to decrease in illumination but is still more than half full. This phase is characterized by gratitude, introspection, and the initial stages of releasing. It is a time to acknowledge the growth and achievements made during the waxing phases and to express gratitude for these accomplishments.

- **Waning Crescent Phase**: As the Moon continues to wane, it enters the Waning Crescent phase, also known as the Balsamic Moon. In this phase, only a small sliver of the Moon is visible. The Waning Crescent phase is a period of deep reflection, rest, and preparation for the New Moon. It is an ideal time to let go of any remaining attachments or burdens and to rest and rejuvenate in preparation for new beginnings.

Utilizing Hemp for Relaxation and Introspection

The waning phases are perfect for relaxation and introspection. Hemp products can enhance these practices by promoting calmness and supporting a reflective state of mind.

- **CBD Oil for Relaxation**: CBD oil is renowned for its relaxing properties. During the waning phases, incorporate CBD oil into your evening routine to help unwind and prepare for introspection. Take a few drops under your tongue or add it to a calming herbal tea before bedtime.

- **Hemp-Infused Tea**: Drinking hemp-infused herbal tea can enhance relaxation and promote a sense of tranquility. Choose blends that include calming herbs like chamomile, lavender, and valerian root. Sip this tea during your evening reflection time or before meditation.
- **CBD Bath Bombs**: A warm bath with a CBD-infused bath bomb can be incredibly soothing. The combination of warm water and CBD can help relax your muscles, ease tension, and create a peaceful environment for reflection. Add calming essential oils, like lavender or eucalyptus, for an enhanced experience.
- **Hemp Candles**: Light hemp-infused candles to create a serene atmosphere. The gentle scent of hemp can help soothe your senses and promote a calming ambiance. Use these candles during meditation, journaling, or any reflective practice.
- **CBD Capsules**: For consistent relaxation and introspection, consider taking CBD capsules as part of your daily routine. These capsules can help maintain a balanced state of mind and support ongoing relaxation and reflection.

Methods for Releasing and Letting Go

The waning phases are an opportune time to release and let go of what no longer serves us. Here are some effective methods for releasing and letting go during these phases:

- **Journaling**: Use a hemp journal to write down any thoughts, emotions, or experiences you want to release. Reflect on the past lunar cycle and identify areas of your life that need letting go. Writing can be a therapeutic way to process and release pent-up emotions.
- **Burning Ritual**: Write down negative thoughts, habits, or situations on a piece of paper. Safely burn the paper using a hemp candle, visualizing the release of these burdens from your life. As

the paper turns to ash, imagine the negative energy dissipating and leaving you feeling lighter and freer.

- **Meditation and Visualization**: Practice guided meditations focused on releasing and letting go. Visualize a gentle stream of light washing away any negativity or attachments. Imagine yourself letting go of these burdens and feeling a sense of peace and renewal. Use hemp products like CBD oil or hemp-infused tea to enhance your meditation experience.

- **Breathwork**: Engage in breathwork exercises to release tension and stress. Practice deep breathing techniques, inhaling deeply through your nose and exhaling slowly through your mouth. Focus on each breath, and with each exhale, visualize releasing any negative energy or stress. Incorporate CBD products to help relax your body and mind during breathwork sessions.

- **Physical Activity**: Engage in gentle physical activities like yoga, tai chi, or walking in nature. These activities can help release physical and emotional tension, promoting a sense of well-being and balance. Use CBD topicals on any areas of tension to enhance the relaxation effects.

- **Gratitude Practice**: Cultivate a gratitude practice by acknowledging and appreciating the positive aspects of your life. Each evening, write down things you are grateful for in a hemp journal. This practice can shift your focus from negativity to positivity, making it easier to release what no longer serves you.

- **Energy Healing**: Explore energy healing practices such as Reiki or crystal healing. These practices can help balance your energy and facilitate the release of negative emotions and blockages. Use hemp-based products, like CBD-infused lotions, to enhance the healing process.

- **Decluttering**: Physically declutter your space as a symbolic act of letting go. Remove items that no longer bring you joy or serve a purpose. This process can create a sense of clarity and open up space for new energy and opportunities. Use hemp-based cleaning products for an eco-friendly approach.

In this chapter, we have explored the significance of the Waning Gibbous and Waning Crescent phases, the benefits of utilizing hemp for relaxation and introspection, and various methods for releasing and letting go. By incorporating hemp into your waning phase rituals, you can enhance your ability to reflect, release, and prepare for new beginnings. As we continue our journey through this book, we will discover more ways to integrate hemp and astrology for holistic healing and personal growth.

Check out my Virtual dispensary for all your hemp needs: https://shift.store/sg1fan23477/retail

Chapter 8: Solar Eclipses and Hemp
Understanding Solar Eclipses and Their Impact

A solar eclipse is a powerful celestial event that occurs when the Moon passes between the Earth and the Sun, temporarily blocking the Sun's light. There are three types of solar eclipses: total, partial, and annular. Each type has its own unique visual and energetic impact.

- **Total Solar Eclipse**: During a total solar eclipse, the Moon completely covers the Sun, casting a shadow over the Earth and turning day into night for a brief period. This rare event has a profound impact on energy and emotions, often symbolizing dramatic changes and new beginnings.
- **Partial Solar Eclipse**: In a partial solar eclipse, only a portion of the Sun is obscured by the Moon. This type of eclipse brings subtle changes and adjustments, influencing our lives in more nuanced ways.
- **Annular Solar Eclipse**: An annular solar eclipse occurs when the Moon is too far from the Earth to completely cover the Sun, creating a "ring of fire" effect. This type of eclipse represents incomplete or gradual transformations.

Solar eclipses are significant in astrology because they occur near the lunar nodes, which are points where the Moon's orbit intersects the ecliptic plane. These nodes are associated with destiny, karma, and life purpose. Eclipses often bring about sudden changes, revelations, and shifts in perspective, making them powerful catalysts for transformation.

- **Astrological Impact**: Solar eclipses can trigger significant events and turning points in our lives. They are often associated with endings and beginnings, highlighting areas where we need to let go of the old to make way for the new. Eclipses can bring hidden issues to light, prompting us to face truths and make necessary changes.
- **Emotional and Energetic Effects**: The intense energy of a solar eclipse can heighten emotions and create a sense of urgency. People may experience heightened sensitivity, restlessness, and a desire for change. This energy can be challenging but also provides an opportunity for growth and transformation.

Special Hemp-Based Practices During Solar Eclipses

Harnessing the unique energy of a solar eclipse can be enhanced through the use of hemp-based practices. Incorporating hemp into your eclipse rituals can help you stay grounded, focused, and open to transformation.

- **Eclipse Meditation with CBD**: Meditation during a solar eclipse can help you align with its transformative energy. Use CBD oil to promote relaxation and clarity. Take a few drops of CBD oil under your tongue before meditating. Find a quiet space, close your eyes, and focus on your breath. Visualize the eclipse's energy surrounding you, illuminating hidden aspects of your life and guiding you toward necessary changes.
- **Hemp-Infused Herbal Tea for Reflection**: Drinking hemp-infused herbal tea can enhance your reflection and introspection during an eclipse. Choose a blend that includes calming herbs like chamomile and lavender, combined with hemp. Sip the tea slowly while journaling about your thoughts and feelings. Reflect on areas of your life that need transformation and set intentions for new beginnings.

- **Eclipse Ritual Bath with CBD Bath Bombs**: A ritual bath during a solar eclipse can help cleanse and rejuvenate your body and spirit. Use a CBD-infused bath bomb to enhance the experience. Fill your bathtub with warm water, add the bath bomb, and immerse yourself. As you soak, visualize the eclipse's energy washing away old patterns and making space for new growth.

- **Grounding Practices with Hemp Products**: The intense energy of a solar eclipse can sometimes feel overwhelming. Grounding practices can help you stay centered. Use hemp-based products like CBD balms or lotions to massage your feet and lower legs. This physical touch can help ground your energy and keep you connected to the Earth.

- **Crystal Healing with Hemp String**: Use crystals that resonate with the transformative energy of a solar eclipse, such as black tourmaline, labradorite, and moonstone. Wrap these crystals in hemp string to create talismans or wear them as jewelry. Hold the crystals or place them on your body during meditation to enhance their energy.

- **Intention Setting with Hemp Journals**: Solar eclipses are powerful times for setting intentions. Use a hemp journal to write down your goals and aspirations. Be specific about the changes you want to manifest in your life. Revisit these intentions regularly to stay focused and committed to your path.

Historical Perspectives and Modern Applications

Solar eclipses have captivated humanity for centuries, inspiring awe, fear, and reverence. Ancient cultures often viewed eclipses as significant omens and incorporated them into their spiritual and religious practices.

- **Ancient China**: In ancient China, solar eclipses were believed to be caused by celestial dragons devouring the Sun. Eclipses were considered powerful omens that could influence the fate of the emperor and the kingdom. Special rituals and ceremonies were performed to appease the dragons and restore balance.

- **Mesoamerican Cultures**: The Mayans and Aztecs closely observed solar eclipses and incorporated them into their complex calendars. They believed eclipses were times of great change and transformation. Eclipses were often associated with the gods and were seen as opportunities to realign with cosmic forces.

- **Ancient Greece and Rome**: In ancient Greece and Rome, solar eclipses were interpreted as signs from the gods. They were believed to foreshadow significant events, such as the death of a ruler or the outbreak of war. Eclipses were often recorded and studied by astronomers and astrologers.

- **Modern Applications**: Today, solar eclipses continue to be significant in astrology and spirituality. They are viewed as powerful opportunities for personal growth and transformation. Many people participate in eclipse rituals and ceremonies to harness the energy of these celestial events.

In this chapter, we have explored the significance of solar eclipses in astrology, the benefits of incorporating hemp into eclipse rituals, and historical perspectives and modern applications. By understanding the transformative energy of solar eclipses and utilizing hemp-based practices, you can enhance your personal growth and spiritual connection. As we continue our journey through this book, we will discover more ways to integrate hemp and astrology for holistic healing and personal transformation.

Check out my Virtual dispensary for all your hemp needs: https://shift.store/sg1fan23477/retail

Chapter 9: Lunar Eclipses and Emotional Healing
The Effects of Lunar Eclipses on Emotions

A lunar eclipse occurs when the Earth passes between the Sun and the Moon, casting a shadow on the Moon and causing it to appear red or darkened. This event, often referred to as a "Blood Moon," carries significant astrological and emotional weight.

- **Astrological Significance**: Lunar eclipses are powerful full moons that occur near the lunar nodes, points of destiny and karma. They signify culminations, revelations, and turning points. Emotions are heightened, and unresolved issues may come to the surface, demanding attention and resolution.
- **Emotional Impact**: The energy of a lunar eclipse can be intense and transformative. It often brings hidden emotions to light, forcing us to confront our deepest feelings. This can lead to emotional breakthroughs and healing, but it can also feel overwhelming. The eclipse can reveal truths about relationships, personal patterns, and life situations that need to change.
- **Shadow Work**: Lunar eclipses are ideal times for shadow work, the process of exploring and integrating the darker, often hidden aspects of ourselves. This work can lead to profound emotional healing and self-awareness, helping us to release old patterns and embrace our true selves.

Hemp for Emotional Balance During Lunar Eclipses

The intense energy of a lunar eclipse can create emotional turbulence, making it essential to find tools that promote emotional balance and support. Hemp products, particularly those containing CBD, can play a crucial role in maintaining emotional equilibrium during these powerful times.

- **CBD Oil for Emotional Calm**: CBD oil is known for its ability to reduce anxiety and promote a sense of calm. During a lunar eclipse, taking CBD oil can help manage heightened emotions and stress. Administer a few drops under the tongue or add them to a calming beverage like herbal tea.
- **Hemp-Infused Herbal Tea**: Drinking hemp-infused herbal tea can provide a soothing effect, helping to calm the mind and body. Choose blends that include herbs like chamomile, lavender, and lemon balm, which are known for their relaxing properties. Sip this tea during the eclipse to support emotional balance.
- **CBD Gummies for Relaxation**: CBD gummies offer a convenient and tasty way to incorporate CBD into your routine. These edibles can help reduce stress and promote relaxation. Consume them in the evening or whenever you feel emotionally overwhelmed during the eclipse.
- **Hemp Candles for Atmosphere**: Create a calming atmosphere with hemp-infused candles. The gentle scent of hemp can help soothe the senses and create a peaceful environment. Light these candles during your lunar eclipse rituals to enhance the ambiance and support emotional healing.
- **CBD Topicals for Tension Relief**: Physical tension often accompanies emotional stress. Using CBD topicals like balms or lotions can help alleviate physical discomfort and promote relaxation. Apply these products to areas of tension, such as the neck and shoulders, to enhance emotional well-being.

Rituals

Personal experiences and rituals during a lunar eclipse can provide valuable insights and inspiration for emotional healing. Here are some detailed personal anecdotes and suggested rituals to harness the energy of a lunar eclipse.

Rituals for Emotional Healing During Lunar Eclipses

- **Lunar Eclipse Meditation**: Find a quiet space where you can sit comfortably. Light hemp-infused candles and apply a few drops of CBD oil under your tongue. Close your eyes and focus on your breath. Visualize the lunar eclipse's energy surrounding you, illuminating your deepest emotions and hidden truths. Allow any thoughts and feelings to surface without judgment. Embrace these revelations and set intentions for emotional healing and growth.

- **Shadow Work Journaling**: Use a hemp journal to explore your shadow self. Write about your fears, insecurities, and unresolved emotions. Reflect on past experiences that still affect you and how you can release these burdens. The act of writing can help you process and integrate these aspects of yourself, leading to greater self-awareness and emotional healing.

- **Ritual Bath for Cleansing and Release**: Prepare a warm bath with a CBD-infused bath bomb. Add calming essential oils like lavender or eucalyptus. As you soak, visualize the water cleansing away negative emotions and old patterns. Reflect on what you need to release and let go of. After your bath, write down anything you wish to release on a piece of paper and burn it safely, symbolizing the letting go of these burdens.

- **Crystal Healing with Hemp**: Use crystals that resonate with the emotional healing energy of a lunar eclipse, such as moonstone, rose quartz, and amethyst. Create a crystal grid using hemp string or hold the crystals during meditation. Focus on the eclipse's energy amplifying the healing properties of the crystals, helping you release emotional blockages and find inner peace.

- **Group Ritual for Support and Healing**: Gather with friends or a supportive community for a lunar eclipse ritual. Create a sacred circle, light hemp-infused candles, and share your intentions and experiences. Perform a guided meditation or group journaling exercise focused on emotional healing and release. The collective energy can amplify the eclipse's power and provide a sense of connection and support.

- **Gratitude and Forgiveness Ritual**: Use the energy of the lunar eclipse to practice gratitude and forgiveness. Write down things you are grateful for and people or situations you need to forgive in a hemp journal. Reflect on the positive aspects of your life and the lessons learned from challenging experiences. Embrace forgiveness as a way to release emotional burdens and create space for healing.

In this chapter, we have explored the effects of lunar eclipses on emotions, the benefits of using hemp for emotional balance during these powerful events and rituals for emotional healing. By understanding the transformative energy of lunar eclipses and incorporating hemp-based practices, you can enhance your emotional well-being and facilitate profound healing. As we continue our journey through this book, we will discover more ways to integrate hemp and astrology for holistic healing and personal transformation.

Check out my Virtual dispensary for all your hemp needs: https://shift.store/sg1fan23477/retail

Chapter 10: The Sun's Influence in Astrology
The Role of the Sun in the Zodiac

In astrology, the Sun is a central and vital influence, often considered the most significant celestial body in the astrological chart. It represents the core of our being, our essence, and our life force. The Sun governs our individuality, our conscious mind, and our sense of self. It is the driving force behind our actions and the source of our vitality and creativity.

- **Astrological Significance**: The Sun's position in the zodiac at the time of our birth determines our Sun sign, also known as the star sign. This sign reflects our fundamental character, our aspirations, and our core identity. Each of the twelve zodiac signs expresses the Sun's energy in a unique way:
  - **Aries**: Dynamic, pioneering, and courageous.
  - **Taurus**: Steady, practical, and sensual.
  - **Gemini**: Communicative, curious, and adaptable.
  - **Cancer**: Nurturing, intuitive, and protective.
  - **Leo**: Confident, creative, and generous.
  - **Virgo**: Analytical, meticulous, and helpful.
  - **Libra**: Harmonious, diplomatic, and sociable.
  - **Scorpio**: Intense, passionate, and transformative.
  - **Sagittarius**: Optimistic, adventurous, and philosophical.
  - **Capricorn**: Ambitious, disciplined, and practical.
  - **Aquarius**: Innovative, humanitarian, and independent.
  - **Pisces**: Compassionate, imaginative, and empathetic.
- **Personal Expression**: The Sun sign is a reflection of how we express ourselves and interact with the world. It influences our goals, our approach to challenges, and our overall life path.

Understanding our Sun sign can provide insights into our strengths, weaknesses, and inherent potential.

- **The Sun's Cycle**: The Sun takes approximately one year to travel through all twelve zodiac signs, spending about a month in each sign. This cycle influences not only individual horoscopes but also the collective energy and themes present during different times of the year.

Hemp Products for Vitality and Energy

Hemp products can enhance our vitality and energy, supporting the dynamic and life-affirming influence of the Sun. Here are some hemp-based products that can help you harness and sustain your energy levels:

- **Hemp Protein Powder**: Hemp protein powder is a complete plant-based protein source that provides essential amino acids, omega-3 and omega-6 fatty acids, and fiber. It is an excellent addition to smoothies and shakes, offering sustained energy and aiding muscle recovery. Use hemp protein powder as part of your daily diet to maintain vitality and support physical activity.
- **CBD Energy Drinks**: CBD-infused energy drinks combine the benefits of CBD with natural stimulants like caffeine and B-vitamins. These drinks can provide a balanced boost of energy without the jitters or crashes associated with traditional energy drinks. Consume a CBD energy drink in the morning or before a workout to enhance focus and endurance.
- **Hemp Seed Oil**: Rich in essential fatty acids, vitamins, and anti-oxidants, hemp seed oil can be used as a nutritional supplement to support overall health and vitality. Add a tablespoon of hemp seed oil to salads, smoothies, or soups to boost your energy levels and improve your well-being.
- **CBD Capsules**: CBD capsules offer a convenient way to in-corporate CBD into your daily routine. They can help manage stress, improve sleep quality, and support a balanced state of

mind, all of which contribute to sustained energy and vitality. Take CBD capsules as part of your morning or evening regimen for consistent benefits.

- **Hemp-Infused Snacks**: Healthy snacks infused with hemp, such as energy bars, granola, or trail mix, provide a nutritious and convenient option for maintaining energy levels throughout the day. These snacks are often packed with protein, fiber, and healthy fats, making them ideal for on-the-go energy.
- **Hemp Topicals for Muscle Relief**: Physical activity is essential for maintaining vitality, and hemp-based topicals like CBD balms and creams can aid in muscle recovery and relief from soreness. Apply these topicals to muscles and joints after exercise to support recovery and maintain an active lifestyle.

Seasonal Changes and the Sun's Path

The Sun's journey through the zodiac and its influence on seasonal changes play a significant role in shaping our experiences and energy levels throughout the year. Understanding the Sun's path can help us align with natural rhythms and harness its energy effectively.

- **Spring (Aries, Taurus, Gemini)**: As the Sun moves through Aries, Taurus, and Gemini, we experience the renewal and growth of spring. This season is associated with new beginnings, increased energy, and the blossoming of ideas and projects. Embrace the vitality of spring by setting new goals and engaging in activities that invigorate your body and mind. Incorporate hemp products like CBD energy drinks and hemp protein shakes to sustain your energy levels during this dynamic season.
- **Summer (Cancer, Leo, Virgo)**: The summer months, governed by Cancer, Leo, and Virgo, bring warmth, abundance, and peak vitality. This is a time for creativity, self-expression, and enjoying the fruits of your labor. Use the Sun's energy to enhance your physical activities, social interactions, and creative pursuits.

Hemp-infused snacks and CBD capsules can help you maintain balanced energy and support an active lifestyle during the high-energy summer months.

- **Autumn (Libra, Scorpio, Sagittarius)**: As the Sun transitions through Libra, Scorpio, and Sagittarius, we enter the reflective and transformative season of autumn. This is a period of harvesting, introspection, and preparing for the colder months ahead. Focus on balancing your energy, nurturing relationships, and exploring deeper aspects of your life. Hemp seed oil and CBD oil can support emotional balance and vitality as you navigate the transitional energy of autumn.

- **Winter (Capricorn, Aquarius, Pisces)**: During the winter months, when the Sun moves through Capricorn, Aquarius, and Pisces, we experience a time of rest, reflection, and inner growth. This season encourages us to slow down, conserve energy, and focus on long-term goals. Use the introspective energy of winter to recharge and plan for the future. Incorporate hemp-infused herbal teas and CBD topicals into your self-care routine to promote relaxation and support overall well-being.

Practical Applications and Exercises

To effectively harness the Sun's energy and incorporate hemp products into your routine, consider the following practical applications and exercises:

- **Morning Routine with Hemp**: Start your day with a nourishing breakfast that includes hemp protein powder or hemp seed oil. Follow with a CBD energy drink or capsules to enhance focus and energy for the day ahead. Incorporate a morning exercise routine, such as yoga or jogging, to align with the Sun's invigorating energy.

- **Seasonal Intentions**: Set intentions at the beginning of each season based on the Sun's position in the zodiac. Use a hemp journal to write down your goals and aspirations for the upcoming months. Reflect on your progress regularly and adjust your intentions as needed.

- **Sun Salutations**: Practice Sun Salutations (Surya Namaskar) as part of your daily exercise routine. This series of yoga poses is designed to honor the Sun and enhance physical vitality. Use CBD topicals to soothe muscles and joints after your practice.
- **Nature Walks**: Spend time outdoors in nature, especially during the changing seasons. Walks in the sunshine can boost your mood and energy levels. Carry hemp-infused snacks for sustained energy during your outings.
- **Seasonal Cleanses**: Perform seasonal cleanses to align with the Sun's energy and support your body's natural rhythms. Incorporate hemp seed oil and hemp-based supplements into your cleanse to promote detoxification and vitality.
- **Creative Projects**: Use the Sun's energy to fuel your creative projects. Whether it's writing, painting, or crafting, engage in activities that allow you to express your individuality and creativity. Use hemp-infused products like candles and essential oils to create a conducive environment for creativity.

In this chapter, we have explored the significant role of the Sun in astrology, the benefits of hemp products for vitality and energy, and the influence of seasonal changes and the Sun's path. By understanding the Sun's impact on our lives and incorporating hemp into our routines, we can enhance our vitality, align with natural rhythms, and achieve a balanced and fulfilling life. As we continue our journey through this book, we will discover more ways to integrate hemp and astrology for holistic healing and personal growth.

Check out my Virtual dispensary for all your hemp needs: https://shift.store/sg1fan23477/retail

Chapter 11: Solar Flares and Hemp's Protective Qualities
What Are Solar Flares and How They Affect Us

Solar flares are powerful bursts of radiation originating from the Sun's surface, often associated with sunspots and magnetic activity. These flares release vast amounts of energy, including electromagnetic radiation and charged particles, into space. While most of this radiation is absorbed by the Earth's atmosphere and magnetic field, solar flares can still have significant impacts on our planet and our well-being.

- **Types of Solar Flares**: Solar flares are classified into categories based on their intensity, with X-class flares being the most intense, followed by M-class, C-class, and B-class flares. X-class flares can cause widespread disruptions, while lower-class flares have more localized effects.
- **Impacts on Earth**: Solar flares can affect the Earth in several ways:
  - **Geomagnetic Storms**: The charged particles from solar flares can interact with the Earth's magnetic field, causing geomagnetic storms. These storms can disrupt power grids, communication systems, and GPS navigation.
  - **Radiation Exposure**: High levels of radiation from intense solar flares can pose risks to astronauts, aviation crews, and passengers on high-altitude flights, especially near the polar regions.
  - **Auroras**: One of the more visually striking effects of solar flares is the enhancement of auroras (Northern and Southern Lights), which are caused by the interaction of solar particles with the Earth's atmosphere.
- **Effects on Human Health and Behavior**: Solar flares can also influence human health and behavior:
  - **Electromagnetic Sensitivity**: Some individuals report symptoms such as headaches, fatigue, irritability, and sleep disturbances during periods of intense solar activity. These

symptoms are believed to be caused by the increased levels of electromagnetic radiation.

- **Mood and Mental State**: The fluctuations in the Earth's magnetic field during solar flares can affect our mood and mental state. Some studies suggest a correlation between geomagnetic storms and increased rates of anxiety, depression, and even heart attacks.

Using Hemp to Mitigate the Effects of Solar Flares

Hemp, particularly products containing CBD (cannabidiol), can play a role in mitigating the adverse effects of solar flares on our well-being. Here are some ways hemp can help:

- **Reducing Anxiety and Stress**: CBD has been shown to have anxiolytic (anxiety-reducing) properties. During periods of intense solar activity, taking CBD oil can help manage stress and anxiety. The calming effects of CBD can counteract the agitation and irritability that some people experience during solar flares.
- **Improving Sleep Quality**: Solar flares can disrupt sleep patterns, leading to insomnia and restlessness. CBD has been found to promote better sleep by regulating the sleep-wake cycle and reducing anxiety. Using CBD oil or capsules before bedtime can help improve sleep quality and duration.
- **Alleviating Physical Discomfort**: Headaches and muscle tension are common complaints during geomagnetic storms. CBD topicals, such as balms and creams, can be applied to areas of discomfort to provide relief. The anti-inflammatory properties of CBD can help reduce pain and tension.
- **Enhancing Overall Well-Being**: Regular use of hemp products can support overall well-being by promoting balance and homeostasis in the body. CBD interacts with the endocannabinoid system, which plays a role in regulating various physiological processes, including mood, sleep, and immune function.

Scientific Insights and Holistic Practices

Scientific research and holistic practices can provide a deeper understanding of how to effectively use hemp to mitigate the effects of solar flares. Here are some insights and practices to consider:

Scientific Insights

- **Endocannabinoid System and CBD**: The endocannabinoid system (ECS) is a complex cell-signaling system that plays a role in regulating a wide range of functions, including mood, sleep, appetite, and immune response. CBD interacts with the ECS by influencing the activity of cannabinoid receptors, such as CB1 and CB2, which are found throughout the body. This interaction helps maintain balance and can mitigate the adverse effects of solar flares.
- **Studies on CBD and Anxiety**: Research has shown that CBD has significant potential in reducing anxiety and stress. For example, a 2019 study published in "The Permanente Journal" found that CBD reduced anxiety levels in a group of participants with anxiety and sleep disorders. These findings suggest that CBD can be an effective tool for managing anxiety during periods of intense solar activity.
- **Sleep Improvement**: Several studies have demonstrated the positive effects of CBD on sleep. A 2017 review in "Current Psychiatry Reports" highlighted that CBD could improve REM sleep behavior disorder and excessive daytime sleepiness. This evidence supports the use of CBD to improve sleep quality during solar flares.

Holistic Practices

- **Daily CBD Routine**: Incorporate CBD into your daily routine to support overall well-being. Start your day with a dose of CBD oil to promote a sense of calm and balance. Use CBD capsules or edibles for sustained effects throughout the day. In the evening, take CBD oil or tincture to unwind and prepare for restful sleep.

- **Meditation and Mindfulness**: Practice meditation and mindfulness techniques to reduce stress and enhance your mental state during solar flares. Use CBD oil to deepen your meditation practice by promoting relaxation and focus. Set aside time each day to meditate, focusing on your breath and allowing any tension or anxiety to melt away.

- **Physical Activity**: Engage in regular physical activity to boost your mood and reduce the physical discomfort associated with solar flares. Activities such as yoga, tai chi, and walking can help alleviate tension and promote a sense of well-being. Apply CBD topicals to sore muscles before and after exercise to enhance recovery and reduce pain.

- **Hydration and Nutrition**: Maintain proper hydration and nutrition to support your body's resilience to the effects of solar flares. Drink plenty of water and consume a balanced diet rich in fruits, vegetables, and whole grains. Incorporate hemp-based foods, such as hemp seeds and hemp protein powder, to provide essential nutrients and support overall health.

- **Grounding Techniques**: Practice grounding techniques to stay connected to the Earth's energy and reduce the impact of solar flares. Spend time outdoors, walking barefoot on grass or sand to ground yourself. Use hemp-infused products like lotions and oils during grounding practices to enhance the experience.

In this chapter, we have explored the nature of solar flares, their effects on our well-being, and how hemp can help mitigate these effects. By understanding the science behind hemp's protective qualities and incorporating holistic practices, we can enhance our resilience to the challenges posed by solar flares. As we continue our journey through this book, we will discover more ways to integrate hemp and astrology for holistic healing and personal growth.

Check out my Virtual dispensary for all your hemp needs: https://shift.store/sg1fan23477/retail

Chapter 12: Mercury and Communication
Mercury's Role in Astrology

Mercury, the smallest planet in our solar system, holds significant influence in astrology. Named after the Roman messenger god, Mercury governs communication, intellect, and technology. Its swift orbit around the Sun, taking only 88 days, reflects its dynamic and versatile nature.

- **Astrological Significance**: Mercury's position in the natal chart reveals how we think, communicate, and process information. It influences our learning style, decision-making abilities, and the way we express ourselves verbally and in writing. Mercury's placement can highlight our mental agility, adaptability, and approach to problem-solving.
- **Ruling Signs**: Mercury rules two zodiac signs: Gemini and Virgo.
    - **Gemini**: In Gemini, Mercury manifests as curiosity, adaptability, and a love for communication. Individuals with strong Mercury influence in Gemini are often quick-witted, sociable, and versatile.
    - **Virgo**: In Virgo, Mercury's influence is seen in analytical thinking, precision, and attention to detail. Those with Mercury in Virgo are often methodical, practical,

and highly efficient in their communication and thought processes.

- **Mercury Retrograde**: Mercury retrograde is a well-known astrological phenomenon where the planet appears to move backward in its orbit. This period, lasting about three weeks and occurring three to four times a year, is often associated with disruptions in communication, technology, and travel. While Mercury retrograde can be challenging, it also offers opportunities for reflection, review, and revisiting unresolved issues.

Hemp for Enhancing Communication and Mental Clarity

Hemp products, particularly those containing CBD, can enhance communication and mental clarity by promoting relaxation, reducing anxiety, and supporting cognitive function. Here are some ways hemp can benefit communication and mental clarity:

- **Reducing Anxiety**: Anxiety can hinder effective communication and clear thinking. CBD has anxiolytic properties that can help reduce anxiety and promote a sense of calm. By alleviating anxiety, CBD can enhance your ability to communicate clearly and confidently.
- **Improving Focus and Concentration**: Maintaining focus is essential for clear communication and effective learning. CBD can help improve concentration and mental clarity, making it easier to stay engaged in conversations and tasks.
- **Enhancing Cognitive Function**: CBD's neuroprotective properties support brain health and cognitive function. Regular use of CBD can help enhance memory, problem-solving skills, and overall mental performance.
- **Promoting Relaxation**: A relaxed mind is more open and receptive to new ideas and information. Hemp-infused products, such as teas and oils, can help promote relaxation, making it easier to communicate and process information effectively.

Techniques and Exercises

To harness the benefits of Mercury's influence and hemp's properties, incorporate the following techniques and exercises into your routine:

Mindfulness and Meditation

- **CBD-Infused Meditation**: Incorporate CBD oil into your meditation practice to enhance relaxation and mental clarity. Take a few drops of CBD oil under your tongue before meditating. Find a quiet space, sit comfortably, and focus on your breath. Allow your mind to settle and become more receptive to insights and ideas.
- **Mindful Communication Practice**: Engage in mindfulness exercises that focus on active listening and mindful speaking. Practice being fully present during conversations, paying attention to both verbal and non-verbal cues. Use CBD products to help maintain a calm and focused state of mind.

Journaling and Writing

- **Hemp Journals**: Use a hemp journal to write down your thoughts, ideas, and reflections. Journaling can help clarify your thoughts and improve your communication skills. Set aside time each day to write about your experiences, goals, and insights.
- **Expressive Writing**: Engage in expressive writing exercises to explore your emotions and thoughts. Choose a topic or prompt and write continuously for a set period, without worrying about grammar or structure. This practice can help you access deeper insights and enhance your ability to communicate effectively.

Breathwork and Relaxation

- **Breathwork Exercises:** Practice deep breathing exercises to calm your mind and enhance mental clarity. Inhale deeply through your nose, hold for a few seconds, and exhale slowly through your mouth. Repeat several times to reduce stress and improve focus. Use CBD-infused products to enhance the relaxation benefits of breathwork.

- **Progressive Muscle Relaxation**: Engage in progressive muscle relaxation to release tension and promote a sense of calm. Starting with your feet, tense each muscle group for a few seconds and then relax. Move up through your body, finishing with your face and head. This practice can help reduce anxiety and improve communication.

Cognitive Exercises and Games

- **Brain Games**: Engage in cognitive exercises and games that challenge your mind and enhance cognitive function. Puzzles, crosswords, and memory games can help improve problem-solving skills and mental agility.
- **Language Learning**: Learning a new language can enhance your communication skills and cognitive abilities. Use language learning apps or take classes to expand your linguistic capabilities. Incorporate CBD products to support focus and memory retention during your studies.

Public Speaking and Social Skills

- **Public Speaking Practice**: Practice public speaking to improve your confidence and communication skills. Join a local Toastmasters club or participate in public speaking workshops. Use CBD oil to help manage any anxiety associated with public speaking.
- **Active Listening Exercises**: Engage in active listening exercises with a partner or group. Practice fully focusing on the speaker, avoiding interruptions, and reflecting back what you heard. This

practice can improve your listening skills and enhance your ability to communicate effectively.

In this chapter, we have explored Mercury's role in astrology, the benefits of using hemp for enhancing communication and mental clarity, and various techniques and exercises to support these goals. By understanding Mercury's influence and incorporating hemp products into your routine, you can improve your communication skills, enhance mental clarity, and achieve greater success in both personal and professional interactions. As we continue our journey through this book, we will discover more ways to integrate hemp and astrology for holistic healing and personal growth.

Check out my Virtual dispensary for all your hemp needs: https://shift.store/sg1fan23477/retail

Chapter 13: Venus and Love
The Influence of Venus on Love and Relationships
Venus, named after the Roman goddess of love and beauty, is a celestial body that governs love, relationships, aesthetics, and values. In astrology, Venus's placement in your natal chart reveals how you express affection, your approach to relationships, and what you find attractive and beautiful.

- **Astrological Significance**: Venus symbolizes harmony, pleasure, and the principle of attraction. It influences our romantic inclinations, social interactions, and appreciation of art and beauty. Venus's placement by sign and house in your chart provides insight into your love language, how you seek and give affection, and your relationship preferences.
    - **Venus in Aries**: Bold, passionate, and direct in expressing love.
    - **Venus in Taurus**: Sensual, loyal, and values stability in relationships.
    - **Venus in Gemini**: Communicative, playful, and enjoys mental stimulation.
    - **Venus in Cancer**: Nurturing, empathetic, and seeks emotional security.
    - **Venus in Leo**: Charismatic, generous, and loves grand gestures of affection.
    - **Venus in Virgo**: Practical, attentive, and values meaningful acts of service.
    - **Venus in Libra**: Diplomatic, romantic, and seeks balance and harmony.
    - **Venus in Scorpio**: Intense, passionate, and values deep emotional connections.

- ○ **Venus in Sagittarius**: Adventurous, optimistic, and values freedom in love.
- ○ **Venus in Capricorn**: Reserved, committed, and values long-term stability.
- ○ **Venus in Aquarius**: Innovative, independent, and values unconventional relationships.
- ○ **Venus in Pisces**: Compassionate, dreamy, and values spiritual connections.
- **Relationship Dynamics**: Venus influences the dynamics of relationships, including how we attract partners, our relationship needs, and our approach to love and affection. Understanding Venus's placement in your chart and your partner's chart can provide valuable insights into compatibility and relationship harmony.
- **Aesthetics and Values**: Beyond love and relationships, Venus also governs our sense of aesthetics and personal values. It influences our tastes in art, fashion, and beauty, as well as our preferences for leisure activities and social interactions.

Hemp for Intimacy and Emotional Connection

Hemp products, particularly those containing CBD, can enhance intimacy and emotional connection by promoting relaxation, reducing anxiety, and supporting a balanced mood. Here are some ways hemp can benefit your love life and relationships:

- **Promoting Relaxation**: A relaxed mind and body are essential for intimacy and emotional connection. CBD has calming properties that can help reduce stress and anxiety, allowing you to be more present and connected with your partner.
- **Enhancing Sensory Experience**: Hemp products can heighten your sensory experience, making touch and physical intimacy more enjoyable. CBD-infused lotions and oils can be used

during massages to enhance the tactile experience and promote relaxation.

- **Supporting Emotional Balance**: Emotional balance is crucial for healthy relationships. CBD can help regulate mood, reduce irritability, and promote a sense of well-being. Using CBD products regularly can help you maintain emotional stability and foster a positive relationship dynamic.

- **Boosting Libido**: CBD can also help improve libido by reducing anxiety and increasing blood flow. This can lead to enhanced sexual arousal and satisfaction.

- **Improving Sleep**: Good quality sleep is essential for overall well-being and relationship health. CBD can help improve sleep quality by promoting relaxation and reducing insomnia, leading to better energy levels and mood during the day.

Love Rituals and Recipes

Incorporating hemp into love rituals and recipes can enhance your intimate moments and deepen your emotional connection with your partner. Here are some detailed love rituals and recipes to try:

Love Rituals

- **CBD-Infused Bath Ritual**: Create a relaxing and romantic bath experience for you and your partner. Add CBD bath bombs or bath salts to warm water. Light candles and play soft music to set the mood. Soak together in the bath, enjoying the calming effects of CBD and the intimate atmosphere. Use this time to connect, communicate, and relax together.

- **Massage Ritual with CBD Oil**: Give each other a soothing massage using CBD-infused massage oil. The calming properties of CBD will help relax muscles and enhance the tactile experience. Take turns massaging each other's back, shoulders, and any areas of tension. This ritual can help deepen your physical connection and promote relaxation.

- **Moonlit Meditation**: Perform a meditation together under the light of the moon, particularly during a Full Moon, which is associated with heightened emotions and connection. Use CBD oil to promote relaxation before starting the meditation. Sit together in a comfortable position, hold hands, and focus on your breath. Visualize the moon's energy enhancing your emotional bond and bringing you closer together.
- **Gratitude Journaling**: Set aside time to journal together about the things you appreciate in your relationship. Use a hemp journal and CBD-infused tea to create a calming environment. Write down what you love about each other, memorable moments, and your hopes for the future. Sharing your gratitude can strengthen your emotional connection and bring positivity to your relationship.

Recipes for Intimacy and Connection

- **CBD-Infused Chocolate-Covered Strawberries**
  - **Ingredients:**
    - 1 cup dark chocolate chips
    - 1 tablespoon CBD oil
    - Fresh strawberries
  - **Instructions:**
    - Melt the dark chocolate chips in a double boiler or microwave.
    - Stir in the CBD oil until fully combined.
    - Dip the strawberries into the chocolate, coating them evenly.
    - Place the chocolate-covered strawberries on a baking sheet lined with parchment paper.
    - Refrigerate until the chocolate sets.
    - Enjoy these delicious treats together, sharing bites and savoring the flavors.

- **Hemp-Infused Romantic Dinner**
  - **Appetizer**: Hemp Seed Pesto Crostini
    - Ingredients:
      - 1 cup fresh basil leaves
      - 1/4 cup hemp seeds
      - 1/4 cup grated Parmesan cheese
      - 1/4 cup olive oil
      - 1 clove garlic
      - Salt and pepper to taste
      - Sliced baguette, toasted
    - Instructions:
      - Blend the basil leaves, hemp seeds, Parmesan cheese, olive oil, and garlic in a food processor until smooth.
      - Season with salt and pepper to taste.
      - Spread the hemp seed pesto on toasted baguette slices.
      - Serve as a light and flavorful appetizer.
  - **Main Course**: Lemon Herb Grilled Chicken with Hemp Heart Salad
    - Ingredients:
      - 2 chicken breasts
      - 2 tablespoons olive oil
      - 1 lemon, juiced
      - 2 cloves garlic, minced
      - 1 tablespoon fresh rosemary, chopped
      - Salt and pepper to taste
      - 1 cup mixed greens
      - 1/4 cup hemp hearts
      - 1/4 cup cherry tomatoes, halved
      - 1/4 cup cucumber, sliced
      - Balsamic vinaigrette
    - Instructions:

- Marinate the chicken breasts in olive oil, lemon juice, garlic, rosemary, salt, and pepper for at least 30 minutes.
- Grill the chicken over medium heat until cooked through.
- Toss the mixed greens, hemp hearts, cherry tomatoes, and cucumber with balsamic vinaigrette.
- Serve the grilled chicken alongside the hemp heart salad for a nutritious and satisfying main course.

  ◦ **Dessert**: Hemp-Infused Berry Parfait
    - **Ingredients:**
      - 1 cup Greek yogurt
      - 1/4 cup hemp seeds
      - 1 cup mixed berries (strawberries, blueberries, raspberries)
      - 2 tablespoons honey
      - 1 teaspoon vanilla extract
    - **Instructions:**
      - Mix the Greek yogurt with honey and vanilla extract.
      - Layer the yogurt mixture, mixed berries, and hemp seeds in serving glasses.
      - Repeat the layers until the glasses are filled.
      - Top with a drizzle of honey and a sprinkle of hemp seeds.
      - Enjoy this light and refreshing dessert together.

Love Elixirs

- **CBD-Infused Love Potion**

- ◦ **Ingredients:**
  - 1 cup pomegranate juice
  - 1 cup sparkling water
  - 1 tablespoon lemon juice
  - 1-2 droppers of CBD oil
  - Fresh mint leaves and pomegranate seeds for garnish
- ◦ **Instructions:**
  - Mix the pomegranate juice, sparkling water, lemon juice, and CBD oil in a pitcher.
  - Stir well to combine.
  - Pour into glasses and garnish with fresh mint leaves and pomegranate seeds.
  - Share this refreshing love potion with your partner, toasting to your connection and affection.
- • **Hemp-Infused Relaxation Tea**
  - ◦ **Ingredients:**
    - 1 tablespoon dried chamomile flowers
    - 1 tablespoon dried lavender buds
    - 1 tablespoon dried rose petals
    - 1 teaspoon hemp seeds
    - 2 cups boiling water
    - Honey to taste
  - ◦ **Instructions:**
    - Combine the chamomile, lavender, rose petals, and hemp seeds in a teapot.
    - Pour boiling water over the herbs and let steep for 5-7 minutes.
    - Strain the tea into cups and sweeten with honey to taste.
    - Sip this calming tea together, enjoying a quiet moment of connection and relaxation.

Love Affirmations and Intentions

- **Affirmation Practice**: Set aside time to practice love affirmations together. Write down positive statements about your relationship, such as "Our love grows stronger every day" or "We communicate openly and honestly." Repeat these affirmations aloud to each other, reinforcing your bond and intentions for your relationship.
- **Intention Setting**: Create a ritual to set intentions for your relationship. Use a hemp journal to write down your goals and desires as a couple. Light a hemp-infused candle and share your intentions with each other. Visualize these intentions manifesting in your relationship, and revisit them regularly to stay aligned and connected.

In this chapter, we have explored Venus's influence on love and relationships, the benefits of using hemp for intimacy and emotional connection, and various love rituals and recipes to enhance your romantic life. By understanding Venus's energy and incorporating hemp into your love practices, you can deepen your emotional connection, enhance intimacy, and create a harmonious and fulfilling relationship. As we continue our journey through this book, we will discover more ways to integrate hemp and astrology for holistic healing and personal growth.

Check out my Virtual dispensary for all your hemp needs: https://shift.store/sg1fan23477/retail

Chapter 14: Mars and Action
Mars' Impact on Drive and Ambition
Mars, the red planet named after the Roman god of war, is a symbol of energy, drive, and ambition in astrology. Mars governs our physical vitality, assertiveness, and desire to achieve goals. Its influence is associated with taking action, pursuing desires, and overcoming challenges.

- **Astrological Significance**: Mars's position in your natal chart reveals how you assert yourself, your level of physical energy, and your approach to achieving goals. It influences your ambition, courage, and competitive spirit. Understanding Mars's placement can provide insights into your motivations and how you pursue success.
    - **Mars in Aries**: Dynamic, assertive, and quick to take action. Individuals with Mars in Aries are natural leaders, driven by a strong desire to initiate and conquer.
    - **Mars in Taurus**: Steady, determined, and patient. Mars in Taurus brings a slow but persistent drive, with a focus on achieving tangible results.
    - **Mars in Gemini**: Versatile, curious, and communicative. Those with Mars in Gemini are motivated by intellectual challenges and thrive in dynamic environments.
    - **Mars in Cancer**: Protective, tenacious, and emotionally driven. Mars in Cancer channels its energy into nurturing and defending loved ones.
    - **Mars in Leo**: Confident, charismatic, and creative. Individuals with Mars in Leo are motivated by recognition and the desire to shine in the spotlight.
    - **Mars in Virgo**: Analytical, meticulous, and hardworking. Mars in Virgo brings a focus on precision and efficiency, driving individuals to perfect their skills.

- ◦ **Mars in Libra**: Diplomatic, balanced, and cooperative. Mars in Libra seeks harmony and is motivated by social interactions and partnerships.
- ◦ **Mars in Scorpio**: Intense, passionate, and resourceful. Mars in Scorpio brings a powerful drive to transform and achieve deep, meaningful goals.
- ◦ **Mars in Sagittarius**: Adventurous, optimistic, and freedom-loving. Individuals with Mars in Sagittarius are driven by the pursuit of knowledge and new experiences.
- ◦ **Mars in Capricorn**: Ambitious, disciplined, and goal-oriented. Mars in Capricorn is focused on long-term success and achieving high status.
- ◦ **Mars in Aquarius**: Innovative, independent, and unconventional. Mars in Aquarius drives individuals to challenge norms and pursue progressive goals.
- ◦ **Mars in Pisces**: Compassionate, imaginative, and spiritually driven. Mars in Pisces channels its energy into creative and altruistic pursuits.

- **Action and Assertiveness**: Mars influences how we take action and assert ourselves in various situations. It governs our physical activities, our ability to confront challenges, and our drive to achieve personal and professional goals.
- **Physical Vitality**: Mars also rules physical vitality and stamina. Its influence determines our level of energy and how we channel it into physical activities, sports, and other forms of exertion.

Energizing with Hemp for Physical and Mental Activity

Hemp products, particularly those containing CBD, can play a vital role in enhancing physical and mental activity. By promoting relaxation, reducing stress, and supporting overall well-being, hemp can help you harness Mars's dynamic energy effectively.

- **Boosting Physical Energy**: Hemp-based products like hemp protein powder and CBD energy drinks can provide the nutrients and stimulation needed for physical activity. Hemp protein powder offers a complete source of plant-based protein, essential for muscle recovery and sustained energy. CBD energy drinks combine the benefits of CBD with natural stimulants, providing a balanced boost without the jitters associated with traditional energy drinks.

- **Enhancing Mental Clarity**: CBD has been shown to support cognitive function and improve focus. By reducing anxiety and promoting a calm mind, CBD can help you maintain mental clarity and stay focused on your tasks. Incorporate CBD oil or capsules into your daily routine to enhance your mental performance.

- **Reducing Stress and Anxiety**: Stress and anxiety can deplete your energy and hinder your ability to take action. CBD's anxiolytic properties can help manage stress, allowing you to approach challenges with a clear and calm mind. Regular use of CBD can support emotional balance and resilience.

- **Supporting Physical Recovery**: After intense physical activity, CBD topicals like balms and creams can aid in muscle recovery and reduce inflammation. Apply these products to sore muscles and joints to enhance recovery and maintain your physical vitality.

- **Promoting Restful Sleep**: Adequate rest is essential for maintaining energy and drive. CBD can help improve sleep quality by promoting relaxation and reducing insomnia. Use CBD products before bedtime to ensure restful and restorative sleep.

Stories and Applications

Integrating hemp into your routine can help you harness the energy of Mars and achieve your goals. Here are some stories and applications to inspire you:

Starting a New Fitness Regimen

- **Morning Energy Boost**: Begin your day with a CBD-infused energy drink to boost your energy levels and prepare for a morning workout. The combination of CBD and natural stimulants will provide sustained energy without the crash.
- **Pre-Workout Hemp Protein Shake**: Mix hemp protein powder with almond milk, a banana, and a handful of spinach for a nutritious pre-workout shake. The protein and nutrients will fuel your muscles and support endurance during your workout.
- **Post-Workout Recovery**: After your workout, apply a CBD balm to sore muscles and joints. The anti-inflammatory properties of CBD will aid in recovery and reduce discomfort, allowing you to stay consistent with your fitness regimen.

Enhancing Mental Performance at Work

- **Morning Focus Routine**: Start your workday with a dose of CBD oil to enhance mental clarity and reduce stress. Use CBD capsules for sustained effects throughout the day.
- **Productivity Breaks**: Take short breaks during your workday to engage in breathwork exercises. Inhale deeply through your nose, hold for a few seconds, and exhale slowly through your mouth. This practice, combined with CBD, can help maintain focus and reduce mental fatigue.
- **Evening Wind-Down**: After a productive day, unwind with a CBD-infused herbal tea. The calming effects of CBD will help you relax and prepare for restful sleep, ensuring you wake up refreshed and ready to tackle the next day's challenges.

Pursuing Creative Projects

- **Setting Creative Intentions**: Use a hemp journal to set your creative intentions and goals. Write down your ideas and aspirations, and revisit them regularly to stay motivated.
- **Creating a Relaxing Environment**: Light hemp-infused candles in your workspace to create a calming and inspiring atmosphere. The gentle scent of hemp can enhance your creative focus and relaxation.
- **Enhancing Creative Flow**: Incorporate CBD oil into your routine to reduce anxiety and promote mental clarity. Use this time to engage in creative activities like painting, writing, or crafting, allowing your ideas to flow freely.

Adventurous Activities and Travel

- **Travel Energy Pack**: When embarking on a trip or adventure, pack hemp-infused snacks and CBD capsules. These products can provide sustained energy and reduce travel-related stress and anxiety.
- **Outdoor Adventures**: For activities like hiking, cycling, or exploring nature, carry a CBD-infused energy drink to stay hydrated and energized. Apply CBD topicals to sore muscles after your adventure to support recovery.
- **Evening Relaxation**: After a day of adventure, unwind with a CBD-infused bath. Use CBD bath bombs or salts to create a relaxing and soothing experience, helping you recover and prepare for the next day's activities.

Developing Assertiveness and Leadership Skills

- **Morning Affirmations**: Start your day with positive affirmations to boost your confidence and assertiveness. Write down statements like "I am a strong and capable leader" or "I confidently pursue my goals." Use CBD oil to enhance relaxation and focus during this practice.

- **Public Speaking Practice**: Practice public speaking to improve your leadership skills. Use CBD to manage anxiety and stay calm. Engage in regular public speaking exercises or join a local Toastmasters club to build confidence.

- **Conflict Resolution**: Use mindfulness and CBD to manage stress during conflict resolution. Practice active listening and assertive communication, focusing on finding mutually beneficial solutions. CBD can help you stay calm and clear-headed during challenging conversations.

In this chapter, we have explored Mars's impact on drive and ambition, the benefits of using hemp for physical and mental activity, and various applications and stories to inspire you. By understanding Mars's energy and incorporating hemp products into your routine, you can enhance your vitality, achieve your goals, and navigate challenges with confidence and resilience. As we continue our journey through this book, we will discover more ways to integrate hemp and astrology for holistic healing and personal growth.

Check out my Virtual dispensary for all your hemp needs: https://shift.store/sg1fan23477/retail

Chapter 15: Jupiter and Expansion
The Role of Jupiter in Growth and Expansion

Jupiter, the largest planet in our solar system, is often referred to as the "Great Benefic" in astrology due to its expansive and benevolent influence. Named after the Roman king of the gods, Jupiter governs growth, abundance, wisdom, and higher learning. Its energy is associated with optimism, generosity, and the pursuit of truth and understanding.

- **Astrological Significance**: Jupiter's position in your natal chart reveals where you experience growth, luck, and opportunities for expansion. It influences your approach to learning, travel, philosophy, and spiritual pursuits. Understanding Jupiter's placement can provide insights into your potential for personal and spiritual development.
    - **Jupiter in Aries**: Bold, pioneering, and enthusiastic about new experiences. Jupiter in Aries encourages growth through adventure and taking risks.
    - **Jupiter in Taurus**: Steady, patient, and values material and financial growth. Jupiter in Taurus promotes abundance through practicality and perseverance.
    - **Jupiter in Gemini**: Curious, communicative, and seeks knowledge through diverse experiences. Jupiter in Gemini supports intellectual expansion and learning.
    - **Jupiter in Cancer**: Nurturing, empathetic, and values emotional and familial growth. Jupiter in Cancer fosters

growth through emotional connections and caring for others.

- **Jupiter in Leo**: Confident, creative, and seeks recognition and self-expression. Jupiter in Leo promotes growth through creativity and leadership.

- **Jupiter in Virgo**: Analytical, diligent, and values growth through service and attention to detail. Jupiter in Virgo encourages growth through practical and intellectual pursuits.

- **Jupiter in Libra**: Diplomatic, fair, and seeks growth through relationships and partnerships. Jupiter in Libra supports expansion through harmony and balance.

- **Jupiter in Scorpio**: Intense, transformative, and seeks deep, meaningful growth. Jupiter in Scorpio promotes growth through transformation and exploring the hidden aspects of life.

- **Jupiter in Sagittarius**: Adventurous, philosophical, and seeks wisdom through exploration and learning. Jupiter in Sagittarius encourages growth through travel, higher education, and spiritual pursuits.

- **Jupiter in Capricorn**: Ambitious, disciplined, and seeks growth through hard work and long-term planning. Jupiter in Capricorn promotes growth through achieving high status and material success.

- **Jupiter in Aquarius**: Innovative, independent, and seeks growth through unconventional and progressive means. Jupiter in Aquarius supports expansion through humanitarian efforts and technological advancements.

- **Jupiter in Pisces**: Compassionate, imaginative, and seeks spiritual growth and connection. Jupiter in Pisces encourages growth through empathy, creativity, and spiritual exploration.

- **Expansion and Abundance**: Jupiter's energy is expansive, encouraging us to grow beyond our limitations and seek new opportunities. It brings a sense of optimism and faith, inspiring us to pursue our dreams and aspirations. Jupiter's influence can lead to abundance in various forms, including wealth, knowledge, and personal fulfillment.
- **Wisdom and Higher Learning**: Jupiter governs higher education, philosophy, and spiritual growth. It encourages us to seek truth, wisdom, and a deeper understanding of life. Jupiter's influence can lead to intellectual and spiritual enlightenment, promoting personal and collective growth.

Hemp for Wisdom and Spiritual Growth

Hemp, particularly CBD, can support wisdom and spiritual growth by promoting relaxation, enhancing meditation, and fostering a sense of well-being. Here are some ways hemp can facilitate your journey towards greater wisdom and spiritual expansion:

- **Promoting Relaxation and Calm**: A calm and relaxed mind is essential for spiritual growth and wisdom. CBD's anxiolytic properties can help reduce anxiety and stress, allowing you to focus on your spiritual practices and inner exploration.
- **Enhancing Meditation**: Meditation is a powerful tool for achieving wisdom and spiritual growth. CBD can enhance your meditation practice by promoting relaxation and improving focus. Taking CBD oil before meditation can help you reach a deeper state of mindfulness and connect with your inner self.
- **Supporting Emotional Balance**: Emotional stability is crucial for personal and spiritual development. CBD can help regulate mood and promote emotional balance, allowing you to approach spiritual practices with a clear and open mind.
- **Encouraging Insight and Intuition**: Hemp products can enhance your intuition and insight, helping you gain a deeper

understanding of yourself and the world around you. Regular use of CBD can support your journey towards greater self-awareness and spiritual enlightenment.

- **Improving Sleep Quality**: Adequate rest is essential for overall well-being and spiritual growth. CBD can help improve sleep quality by promoting relaxation and reducing insomnia. A well-rested mind is more receptive to spiritual practices and personal growth.

Expansive Practices and Experiences

To harness Jupiter's energy for growth and expansion, incorporate the following practices and experiences into your routine:

Meditation and Mindfulness

- **CBD-Infused Meditation**: Incorporate CBD oil into your meditation practice to enhance relaxation and focus. Take a few drops of CBD oil under your tongue before meditating. Find a quiet space, sit comfortably, and focus on your breath. Allow your mind to settle and become more receptive to insights and spiritual growth.
- **Gratitude Meditation**: Practice gratitude meditation to cultivate a sense of abundance and appreciation. Use a hemp-infused candle to create a calming atmosphere. Close your eyes, take deep breaths, and reflect on the things you are grateful for. This practice can help shift your mindset towards positivity and expansion.

Higher Learning and Education

- **Pursue Knowledge**: Jupiter encourages the pursuit of knowledge and wisdom. Enroll in courses, attend workshops, or read books on subjects that interest you. Use CBD products to enhance focus and reduce anxiety during your studies.

- **Philosophical Exploration**: Engage in philosophical discussions and explore different perspectives. Join a study group or participate in online forums to expand your understanding of various philosophies and spiritual teachings.

Travel and Exploration

- **Expand Your Horizons**: Travel is a powerful way to experience growth and expansion. Plan trips to new places, whether near or far, to broaden your horizons and gain new experiences. Use CBD-infused snacks and capsules to manage travel-related stress and enhance your adventures.
- **Cultural Immersion**: Immerse yourself in different cultures and traditions to gain a deeper understanding of the world. Participate in cultural events, try new foods, and engage with locals to enrich your experiences.

Spiritual Practices

- **Yoga and Breathwork**: Practice yoga and breathwork to connect with your body and mind. Use CBD topicals to soothe muscles and enhance relaxation during your practice. Focus on poses and breathing techniques that promote expansion and openness.
- **Creative Expression**: Engage in creative activities like painting, writing, or music to express yourself and explore your inner world. Use CBD oil to reduce anxiety and enhance your creative flow.

Personal Development

- **Set Intentions and Goals**: Use a hemp journal to set intentions and goals for your personal and spiritual growth. Write down your aspirations and revisit them regularly to stay focused and motivated.

- **Positive Affirmations**: Practice positive affirmations to reinforce your sense of abundance and growth. Write down affirmations like "I am open to new opportunities" or "I embrace growth and expansion." Repeat these affirmations daily to cultivate a positive mindset.

Community and Service

- **Humanitarian Efforts**: Jupiter's energy encourages generosity and service. Volunteer for causes you care about or participate in community projects. Use CBD products to manage stress and maintain emotional balance while serving others.
- **Building Connections**: Foster connections with like-minded individuals who share your interests and values. Join clubs, attend events, or participate in online communities to build supportive relationships and expand your social network.

Nature and Outdoors

- **Nature Walks and Hikes**: Spend time in nature to connect with the expansive energy of the Earth. Take regular walks or hikes to clear your mind and gain inspiration. Use CBD-infused products to enhance relaxation and enjoyment during your outdoor activities.
- **Gardening and Plant Care**: Engage in gardening or plant care to cultivate a sense of growth and nurturing. Plant herbs, flowers, or vegetables and care for them regularly. Use hemp-based fertilizers to support healthy plant growth.

In this chapter, we have explored Jupiter's role in growth and expansion, the benefits of using hemp for wisdom and spiritual growth, and various expansive practices and experiences to enhance your journey. By understanding Jupiter's energy and incorporating hemp products into your routine, you can foster personal and spiritual growth, achieve greater wisdom, and embrace a life of abundance and expansion. As we continue our journey through this book, we will discover more ways to integrate hemp and astrology for holistic healing and personal growth.

Check out my Virtual dispensary for all your hemp needs: https://shift.store/sg1fan23477/retail

Chapter 16: Saturn and Discipline
Saturn's Influence on Structure and Discipline

Saturn, often referred to as the "taskmaster" of the zodiac, is a planet associated with structure, discipline, and responsibility. Named after the Roman god of agriculture and time, Saturn's influence is integral in shaping our lives through hard work, perseverance, and adherence to rules and boundaries.

- **Astrological Significance**: Saturn's position in your natal chart reveals your approach to discipline, authority, and long-term goals. It governs areas of life where you need to exercise patience, build structures, and face challenges with resilience. Understanding Saturn's placement can provide insights into your areas of greatest responsibility and potential for growth through effort.
    - **Saturn in Aries**: Strong drive for personal achievement and leadership. Challenges involve learning patience and cooperation.
    - **Saturn in Taurus**: Focus on financial stability and material security. Challenges involve overcoming resistance to change and learning flexibility.
    - **Saturn in Gemini**: Emphasis on communication and intellectual discipline. Challenges involve developing consistency and depth in learning.
    - **Saturn in Cancer**: Importance of emotional security and family responsibilities. Challenges involve balancing personal needs with those of loved ones.
    - **Saturn in Leo**: Drive for creative expression and recognition. Challenges involve overcoming pride and learning humility.

- ◦ **Saturn in Virgo**: Emphasis on service, health, and practical skills. Challenges involve overcoming perfectionism and developing self-acceptance.
- ◦ **Saturn in Libra**: Focus on relationships and social responsibilities. Challenges involve finding balance and developing fairness.
- ◦ **Saturn in Scorpio**: Drive for deep transformation and understanding of power dynamics. Challenges involve overcoming fear and learning trust.
- ◦ **Saturn in Sagittarius**: Emphasis on higher learning, travel, and philosophical pursuits. Challenges involve overcoming dogmatism and embracing open-mindedness.
- ◦ **Saturn in Capricorn**: Strong focus on career and long-term goals. Challenges involve overcoming rigidity and learning to balance work with personal life.
- ◦ **Saturn in Aquarius**: Emphasis on innovation and social responsibility. Challenges involve balancing individuality with community needs.
- ◦ **Saturn in Pisces**: Focus on spirituality and compassion. Challenges involve overcoming escapism and developing practical spirituality.

- **Structure and Boundaries**: Saturn is associated with structure and boundaries, teaching us the importance of rules, limitations, and responsibilities. It governs institutions, laws, and societal structures, emphasizing the need for order and discipline in our lives.
- **Lessons and Challenges**: Saturn often brings challenges and lessons that require hard work and perseverance. These challenges are opportunities for growth, helping us develop resilience, maturity, and wisdom. Saturn's influence encourages us to face our fears, overcome obstacles, and achieve long-term success through disciplined effort.

Using Hemp for Grounding and Stability

Hemp, particularly products containing CBD, can support grounding and stability by promoting relaxation, reducing anxiety, and fostering a sense of calm and balance. Here are some ways hemp can help you align with Saturn's energy of discipline and structure:

- **Promoting Relaxation and Calm**: CBD's anxiolytic properties can help reduce stress and anxiety, promoting a sense of calm and relaxation. This is essential for grounding and maintaining focus on long-term goals.
- **Enhancing Focus and Concentration**: CBD can improve mental clarity and focus, helping you stay disciplined and organized. Incorporating CBD into your daily routine can support your ability to concentrate on tasks and responsibilities.
- **Supporting Emotional Balance**: Emotional stability is crucial for maintaining discipline and structure. CBD can help regulate mood and promote emotional balance, allowing you to approach challenges with a clear and composed mind.
- **Improving Sleep Quality**: Adequate rest is essential for overall well-being and the ability to stay disciplined. CBD can help improve sleep quality by promoting relaxation and reducing insomnia. A well-rested mind and body are better equipped to handle responsibilities and maintain focus.
- **Alleviating Physical Discomfort**: Physical discomfort can be a distraction and hinder your ability to stay disciplined. CBD topicals, such as balms and creams, can help alleviate pain and inflammation, allowing you to stay active and productive.

Practical Applications and Examples

To harness Saturn's energy for structure and discipline, incorporate the following practical applications and examples into your routine:

Daily Routines and Rituals

- **Morning CBD Routine**: Start your day with a dose of CBD oil to promote relaxation and focus. Taking CBD in the morning can help you approach your day with a clear mind and a calm demeanor, setting the tone for productivity and discipline.
- **Structured Planning**: Use a hemp journal to plan your daily, weekly, and monthly tasks. Break down your long-term goals into manageable steps and create a structured schedule to stay organized. Review your progress regularly and adjust your plans as needed.
- **Mindfulness Practice**: Incorporate mindfulness practices, such as meditation or breathwork, into your daily routine. Use CBD-infused products to enhance relaxation and focus during these practices. Mindfulness can help you stay grounded and centered, improving your ability to handle responsibilities and challenges.

Work and Productivity

- **Focused Work Sessions**: Use CBD to enhance your focus and concentration during work or study sessions. Set specific goals for each session and use a timer to maintain discipline. Take short breaks between sessions to rest and recharge.
- **Task Prioritization**: Prioritize your tasks based on importance and deadlines. Use CBD to manage stress and maintain a clear mind while prioritizing and tackling your responsibilities. Create a to-do list and check off completed tasks to stay motivated and organized.
- **Physical Activity**: Incorporate regular physical activity into your routine to maintain energy and focus. Use CBD topicals to relieve muscle tension and soreness after exercise. Physical activity can help you stay disciplined and maintain a healthy balance between work and relaxation.

Emotional and Mental Well-Being

- **Journaling for Emotional Balance**: Use a hemp journal to write about your thoughts, feelings, and experiences. Journaling can help you process emotions and gain clarity, promoting emotional stability. Reflect on your challenges and successes, and use CBD to support relaxation and introspection.
- **Stress Management Techniques**: Practice stress management techniques, such as deep breathing, progressive muscle relaxation, or yoga. Use CBD products to enhance the calming effects of these practices. Managing stress is essential for maintaining discipline and staying focused on your goals.
- **Setting Boundaries**: Establish clear boundaries in your personal and professional life to maintain structure and balance. Use CBD to reduce anxiety and enhance your ability to assertively communicate and uphold these boundaries. Boundaries are crucial for preventing burnout and maintaining discipline.

Long-Term Goals and Aspirations

- **Vision Board Creation**: Create a vision board to visualize your long-term goals and aspirations. Use images, quotes, and symbols that represent your ambitions and the discipline required to achieve them. Place your vision board in a prominent location as a daily reminder of your goals.
- **Progress Tracking**: Regularly track your progress toward your long-term goals. Use a hemp journal or planner to record milestones and achievements. Celebrate your successes and use CBD to maintain a positive mindset and resilience in the face of challenges.
- **Accountability Partners**: Partner with someone who shares similar goals and values. Check in with each other regularly to share progress, offer support, and stay accountable. Use CBD products to maintain emotional balance and enhance your ability to communicate effectively.

Spiritual and Personal Growth

- **Meditation for Grounding**: Practice grounding meditation to connect with Saturn's stabilizing energy. Use CBD oil to enhance relaxation and focus during your meditation. Visualize roots growing from your feet into the Earth, anchoring you in stability and discipline.
- **Personal Reflection**: Set aside time for personal reflection and self-assessment. Use a hemp journal to write about your experiences, challenges, and growth. Reflect on how Saturn's influence has shaped your discipline and structure, and use CBD to support relaxation and clarity during this practice.
- **Rituals for Stability**: Create rituals that promote stability and grounding in your life. Light hemp-infused candles, use essential oils, and incorporate CBD into your rituals. These practices can help you stay connected to Saturn's energy and maintain a disciplined and structured approach to life.

In this chapter, we have explored Saturn's influence on structure and discipline, the benefits of using hemp for grounding and stability, and various practical applications and examples to enhance your routine. By understanding Saturn's energy and incorporating hemp products into your daily life, you can develop resilience, maintain focus, and achieve long-term success through disciplined effort. As we continue our journey through this book, we will discover more ways to integrate hemp and astrology for holistic healing and personal growth.

Check out my Virtual dispensary for all your hemp needs: https://shift.store/sg1fan23477/retail

Chapter 17: Uranus and Innovation
Uranus' Impact on Innovation and Change

Uranus, the planet named after the Greek god of the sky, is known for its association with innovation, rebellion, and sudden change. Its influence in astrology is revolutionary, encouraging us to break free from traditional norms and embrace new ideas and technologies. Uranus represents the unconventional, the unexpected, and the visionary.

- **Astrological Significance**: Uranus's position in your natal chart reveals where you seek freedom, originality, and transformation. It governs areas of life where you experience sudden insights, breakthroughs, and a desire for change. Understanding Uranus's placement can provide insights into your approach to innovation, technology, and societal progress.
    - **Uranus in Aries**: Pioneering, bold, and driven to initiate change. Uranus in Aries encourages innovation through direct action and leadership.
    - **Uranus in Taurus**: Groundbreaking in finance and material resources. Uranus in Taurus promotes change in how we value and use resources, focusing on sustainability and innovation.
    - **Uranus in Gemini**: Innovative in communication and information. Uranus in Gemini supports advancements in technology, media, and education.
    - **Uranus in Cancer**: Transformative in home and family dynamics. Uranus in Cancer encourages new approaches to emotional expression and domestic life.
    - **Uranus in Leo**: Creative and revolutionary in self-expression. Uranus in Leo promotes innovation in the arts and personal creativity.

- ◦ **Uranus in Virgo**: Innovative in health and service. Uranus in Virgo supports advancements in medicine, wellness, and environmental sustainability.
- ◦ **Uranus in Libra**: Revolutionary in relationships and social justice. Uranus in Libra encourages new approaches to partnerships and equality.
- ◦ **Uranus in Scorpio**: Transformative in power and deep psychological insights. Uranus in Scorpio promotes innovation in understanding human behavior and societal structures.
- ◦ **Uranus in Sagittarius**: Adventurous and forward-thinking in philosophy and travel. Uranus in Sagittarius supports new ideas in education, spirituality, and global exploration.
- ◦ **Uranus in Capricorn**: Innovative in career and authority. Uranus in Capricorn encourages changes in traditional institutions and leadership styles.
- ◦ **Uranus in Aquarius**: Naturally aligned with its ruling planet. Uranus in Aquarius promotes technological advancements, humanitarian efforts, and social progress.
- ◦ **Uranus in Pisces**: Visionary and creative in spirituality and compassion. Uranus in Pisces supports new approaches to spirituality, art, and collective empathy.
- **Innovation and Change**: Uranus is the planet of sudden shifts and groundbreaking changes. Its energy disrupts the status quo, encouraging us to think outside the box and embrace the future. Uranus fosters innovation in all areas of life, from personal development to societal advancements.
- **Rebellion and Freedom**: Uranus also represents rebellion and the desire for freedom. It challenges restrictive structures and encourages us to seek independence and authenticity. This influence can lead to radical transformations and the breaking of old patterns.

Hemp for Creativity and Breaking Routines

Hemp, particularly products containing CBD, can support creativity and the breaking of routines by promoting relaxation, reducing anxiety, and fostering a sense of openness and flexibility. Here are some ways hemp can help you align with Uranus's energy of innovation and change:

- **Promoting Relaxation and Openness**: CBD's anxiolytic properties can help reduce stress and anxiety, promoting a sense of relaxation and openness to new ideas. This is essential for creative thinking and embracing change.

- **Enhancing Focus and Mental Clarity**: CBD can improve mental clarity and focus, helping you concentrate on creative projects and innovative ideas. Incorporating CBD into your daily routine can support your ability to think critically and solve problems effectively.

- **Supporting Emotional Flexibility**: Emotional stability and flexibility are crucial for adapting to change and breaking routines. CBD can help regulate mood and promote emotional balance, allowing you to approach new situations with a positive and adaptable mindset.

- **Boosting Creative Inspiration**: Hemp products can enhance your creative inspiration by promoting a relaxed and open state of mind. Regular use of CBD can support your creative processes and help you think outside the box.

- **Improving Sleep Quality**: Adequate rest is essential for overall well-being and creativity. CBD can help improve sleep quality by promoting relaxation and reducing insomnia. A well-rested mind is more receptive to innovative ideas and solutions.

Innovative Practices and Examples

To harness Uranus's energy for innovation and change, incorporate the following practices and examples into your routine:

Creative Practices

- **CBD-Infused Creative Sessions**: Incorporate CBD oil into your creative practice to enhance relaxation and focus. Take a few drops of CBD oil under your tongue before engaging in creative activities like painting, writing, or music. Allow yourself to explore new ideas and techniques without judgment.
- **Brainstorming with Hemp**: Use hemp-infused products, such as CBD gummies or tea, during brainstorming sessions. The calming effects of CBD can help reduce anxiety and open your mind to new possibilities. Write down all your ideas, no matter how unconventional, and explore them further.
- **Artistic Exploration**: Engage in artistic exploration by trying new mediums and techniques. Use hemp-based art supplies, such as hemp paper or hemp-based paints, to create your works. Experiment with different styles and approaches to expand your creative horizons.

Breaking Routines

- **Mindfulness and Meditation**: Practice mindfulness and meditation to break free from habitual thinking patterns. Use CBD-infused products to enhance relaxation and focus during these practices. Set aside time each day to meditate and reflect on new ways to approach your routines.
- **Travel and Exploration**: Travel to new places and immerse yourself in different cultures to gain fresh perspectives. Use CBD-infused snacks and capsules to manage travel-related stress and enhance your experiences. Explore new environments and allow yourself to be inspired by the diversity and novelty around you.
- **Physical Activities**: Engage in physical activities that challenge your body and mind. Try new sports or fitness routines, such as yoga, dance, or martial arts. Use CBD topicals to relieve muscle

tension and soreness after exercise. Physical activity can help you break out of old patterns and develop new habits.

Innovative Learning

- **Online Courses and Workshops**: Enroll in online courses and workshops to learn new skills and expand your knowledge. Use CBD products to enhance focus and reduce anxiety during your studies. Explore topics that interest you and challenge your current understanding.
- **Reading and Research**: Read books and articles on innovative ideas and practices. Use CBD to improve concentration and retention. Explore diverse perspectives and incorporate new concepts into your thinking.
- **Networking and Collaboration**: Connect with like-minded individuals who share your passion for innovation. Join online forums, attend virtual events, or participate in collaborative projects. Use CBD to manage social anxiety and enhance your ability to communicate and collaborate effectively.

Technological Innovation

- **Experimenting with Technology**: Embrace new technologies and experiment with innovative tools and platforms. Use hemp-based products to maintain focus and reduce stress while learning and applying new technologies. Stay curious and open to how technology can enhance your personal and professional life.
- **Developing New Solutions**: Apply your creativity and problem-solving skills to develop new solutions for existing challenges. Use CBD to promote a clear and focused mind, allowing you to think critically and innovatively. Test and refine your solutions, seeking feedback and iterating as needed.

Spiritual and Personal Growth

- **Visionary Meditation**: Practice visionary meditation to connect with Uranus's energy of innovation and change. Use CBD oil to enhance relaxation and focus. Visualize yourself breaking free from old patterns and embracing new possibilities. Allow yourself to be guided by your intuition and inner wisdom.
- **Journaling for Innovation**: Use a hemp journal to write about your innovative ideas and aspirations. Set aside time each day to journal about new insights, experiences, and goals. Reflect on how you can apply Uranus's energy to your personal and spiritual growth.
- **Rituals for Change**: Create rituals that celebrate change and innovation in your life. Light hemp-infused candles, use essential oils, and incorporate CBD into your rituals. Focus on embracing new experiences and breaking free from old routines.

In this chapter, we have explored Uranus's impact on innovation and change, the benefits of using hemp for creativity and breaking routines, and various innovative practices and examples to enhance your routine. By understanding Uranus's energy and incorporating hemp products into your daily life, you can foster creativity, embrace change, and develop new habits that support your personal and professional growth. As we continue our journey through this book, we will discover more ways to integrate hemp and astrology for holistic healing and personal development.

Check out my Virtual dispensary for all your hemp needs: https://shift.store/sg1fan23477/retail

Chapter 18: Neptune and Intuition
Neptune's Role in Dreams and Intuition

Neptune, the planet named after the Roman god of the sea, governs the realms of dreams, intuition, spirituality, and illusion. In astrology, Neptune represents the unconscious mind, the mystical, and the transcendental. It is associated with deep intuition, psychic abilities, and the dissolution of boundaries between the physical and spiritual worlds.

- **Astrological Significance**: Neptune's position in your natal chart reveals how you connect with your inner world, your spiritual beliefs, and your intuitive abilities. It influences your dreams, creativity, and sensitivity to subtle energies. Understanding Neptune's placement can provide insights into your spiritual path and intuitive gifts.
    - **Neptune in Aries**: Intuition expressed through action and innovation. Neptune in Aries encourages pioneering spiritual practices and direct intuitive insights.
    - **Neptune in Taurus**: Intuition connected to the material world and sensual experiences. Neptune in Taurus promotes a practical approach to spirituality and a deep connection to nature.
    - **Neptune in Gemini**: Intuition expressed through communication and mental exploration. Neptune in Gemini supports intuitive insights gained through learning and sharing knowledge.
    - **Neptune in Cancer**: Intuition deeply connected to emotions and home. Neptune in Cancer fosters strong psychic abilities and a nurturing approach to spirituality.

- ◦ **Neptune in Leo**: Intuition expressed through creativity and self-expression. Neptune in Leo encourages artistic and dramatic spiritual practices.
- ◦ **Neptune in Virgo**: Intuition grounded in service and health. Neptune in Virgo promotes practical spirituality and intuitive healing practices.
- ◦ **Neptune in Libra**: Intuition expressed through relationships and balance. Neptune in Libra supports intuitive insights into social harmony and partnerships.
- ◦ **Neptune in Scorpio**: Intuition deeply connected to transformation and the unseen. Neptune in Scorpio fosters powerful psychic abilities and a profound understanding of life's mysteries.
- ◦ **Neptune in Sagittarius**: Intuition expressed through exploration and philosophy. Neptune in Sagittarius encourages spiritual journeys and the pursuit of higher knowledge.
- ◦ **Neptune in Capricorn**: Intuition connected to structure and discipline. Neptune in Capricorn promotes practical and disciplined spiritual practices.
- ◦ **Neptune in Aquarius**: Intuition expressed through innovation and humanitarian efforts. Neptune in Aquarius supports progressive and unconventional spiritual insights.
- ◦ **Neptune in Pisces**: Intuition deeply connected to compassion and universal consciousness. Neptune in Pisces fosters profound psychic abilities and a deep sense of empathy.
- **Dreams and Illusions**: Neptune governs the realm of dreams and illusions, blurring the lines between reality and fantasy. Its influence can inspire vivid dreams, imaginative creativity, and spiritual visions. However, Neptune's energy can also lead to confusion, escapism, and deception if not grounded properly.
- **Spirituality and Mysticism**: Neptune's energy is inherently spiritual, encouraging a connection to the divine and the mystical. It

governs practices like meditation, psychic abilities, and spiritual healing. Neptune's influence can help you tap into your higher self and access deeper layers of consciousness.

Enhancing Intuition with Hemp

Hemp, particularly products containing CBD, can support and enhance your intuitive abilities by promoting relaxation, reducing anxiety, and fostering a sense of inner peace. Here are some ways hemp can help you align with Neptune's energy of dreams and intuition:

- **Promoting Relaxation and Calm**: CBD's anxiolytic properties can help reduce stress and anxiety, creating a calm and centered state of mind. This relaxation is essential for tuning into your intuition and accessing deeper layers of consciousness.
- **Enhancing Meditation and Mindfulness**: Meditation is a powerful tool for developing intuition. CBD can enhance your meditation practice by promoting relaxation and focus. Incorporating CBD into your routine can help you reach a deeper state of mindfulness and connect with your inner self.
- **Supporting Emotional Balance**: Emotional stability is crucial for intuitive clarity. CBD can help regulate mood and promote emotional balance, allowing you to approach intuitive practices with a clear and open heart.
- **Improving Sleep and Dream Recall**: Adequate rest is essential for overall well-being and the ability to remember and interpret dreams. CBD can help improve sleep quality by promoting relaxation and reducing insomnia. A well-rested mind is more receptive to intuitive insights and dream messages.
- **Alleviating Physical Discomfort**: Physical discomfort can distract from intuitive practices. CBD topicals, such as balms and creams, can help alleviate pain and inflammation, allowing you to stay focused and connected during spiritual and psychic practices.

Dreamwork and Psychic Practices

To harness Neptune's energy for dreams and intuition, incorporate the following dreamwork and psychic practices into your routine:

Dreamwork

- **CBD-Infused Pre-Sleep Routine**: Incorporate CBD oil into your pre-sleep routine to promote relaxation and enhance dream recall. Take a few drops of CBD oil under your tongue before bedtime. Create a calming environment by dimming the lights, playing soft music, and using essential oils like lavender to relax your mind and body.
- **Dream Journaling**: Keep a hemp journal by your bedside to record your dreams upon waking. Writing down your dreams immediately helps improve recall and provides insights into your subconscious mind. Use CBD to promote relaxation before sleep, enhancing the vividness and clarity of your dreams.
- **Lucid Dreaming Practices**: Lucid dreaming involves becoming aware that you are dreaming while still in the dream state. To enhance your ability to lucid dream, practice reality checks throughout the day and set intentions before sleep. Use CBD to promote relaxation and reduce anxiety, creating a conducive environment for lucid dreaming.
- **Dream Interpretation**: Interpret your dreams by analyzing symbols, themes, and emotions. Use your intuition to uncover the deeper meanings and messages within your dreams. Incorporate CBD into your meditation practice to enhance relaxation and intuitive clarity during dream interpretation.

Psychic Practices

- **Intuitive Meditation**: Practice intuitive meditation to develop your psychic abilities. Use CBD oil to enhance relaxation and focus. Sit in a comfortable position, close your eyes, and focus on your breath. Allow your mind to become quiet and receptive. Pay attention to any intuitive impressions, images, or sensations that arise.

- **Using Divination Tools**: Explore divination tools like tarot cards, runes, or pendulums to enhance your intuition. Use CBD to promote a calm and focused state of mind during your divination practice. Draw cards or runes, and interpret their meanings based on your intuitive insights.

- **Energy Healing and Reiki**: Practice energy healing or Reiki to develop your intuitive abilities and connect with subtle energies. Use CBD to enhance relaxation and focus during your healing sessions. Pay attention to any intuitive impressions you receive while working with energy.

- **Visualization Techniques**: Use visualization techniques to strengthen your psychic abilities. Practice visualizing different scenarios or images in your mind's eye. Use CBD to promote relaxation and clarity during your visualization practice. This can help you develop the ability to receive intuitive images and messages.

Spiritual Practices

- **Chakra Balancing**: Work on balancing your chakras to enhance your intuition and spiritual connection. Use CBD-infused products to promote relaxation and support your chakra balancing practice. Visualize each chakra opening and aligning, allowing energy to flow freely through your body.

- **Connecting with Spirit Guides**: Practice connecting with your spirit guides or higher self for guidance and support. Use CBD to promote relaxation and create a calm environment for your practice. Sit quietly, close your eyes, and invite your spirit guides to communicate with you. Pay attention to any intuitive impressions or messages you receive.

- **Nature Meditation**: Spend time in nature to enhance your intuition and connect with the natural world. Use CBD-infused products to promote relaxation and mindfulness during your nature meditation. Sit quietly in a natural setting, observe your surroundings, and allow yourself to become attuned to the energies of nature.

Creative Practices

- **Artistic Expression**: Engage in artistic activities like painting, drawing, or music to express your intuition and creativity. Use CBD to reduce anxiety and enhance your creative flow. Allow your intuition to guide your artistic expression, and pay attention to any insights or messages that emerge through your art.
- **Automatic Writing**: Practice automatic writing to tap into your subconscious mind and intuitive insights. Use a hemp journal and CBD to promote relaxation and focus. Sit quietly, hold a pen, and allow your hand to move freely across the page without conscious direction. Review your writing for any intuitive messages or insights.
- **Creative Visualization**: Use creative visualization to enhance your intuition and manifest your desires. Use CBD to promote relaxation and clarity during your visualization practice. Close your eyes, visualize your goals and desires in detail, and feel the emotions associated with achieving them. This practice can help you tap into your intuition and align with your higher self.

In this chapter, we have explored Neptune's role in dreams and intuition, the benefits of using hemp for enhancing intuition, and various dreamwork and psychic practices to develop your intuitive abilities. By understanding Neptune's energy and incorporating hemp products into your routine, you can deepen your spiritual connection, enhance your intuitive insights, and access the wisdom of your subconscious mind. As we continue our journey through this book, we will discover more ways to integrate hemp and astrology for holistic healing and personal growth.

Check out my Virtual dispensary for all your hemp needs: https://shift.store/sg1fan23477/retail

Chapter 19: Pluto and Transformation
The Transformative Power of Pluto

Pluto, the distant and enigmatic dwarf planet, is a potent force in astrology. Named after the Roman god of the underworld, Pluto governs transformation, rebirth, and deep psychological processes. Its energy is intense and transformative, pushing us to confront our shadows and emerge renewed and empowered.

- **Astrological Significance**: Pluto's position in your natal chart reveals where you experience profound transformations, power struggles, and opportunities for rebirth. It influences your approach to change, your capacity for psychological insight, and your ability to release old patterns. Understanding Pluto's placement can provide insights into your potential for deep personal growth and healing.
  - **Pluto in Aries**: Transformation through personal power and pioneering action. Pluto in Aries fosters a drive for self-discovery and leadership.
  - **Pluto in Taurus**: Transformation through material security and values. Pluto in Taurus encourages reevaluating your relationship with possessions and stability.
  - **Pluto in Gemini**: Transformation through communication and knowledge. Pluto in Gemini promotes deep intellectual insights and the power of words.
  - **Pluto in Cancer**: Transformation through emotional depth and family dynamics. Pluto in Cancer fosters healing through nurturing and emotional release.

- **Pluto in Leo**: Transformation through creativity and self-expression. Pluto in Leo encourages reclaiming personal power and authenticity.
- **Pluto in Virgo**: Transformation through health and service. Pluto in Virgo promotes healing through practical efforts and attention to detail.
- **Pluto in Libra**: Transformation through relationships and balance. Pluto in Libra fosters deep insights into partnerships and social justice.
- **Pluto in Scorpio**: Transformation through intensity and power. Pluto in Scorpio encourages exploring the depths of the psyche and embracing profound change.
- **Pluto in Sagittarius**: Transformation through exploration and belief systems. Pluto in Sagittarius promotes growth through philosophical insights and travel.
- **Pluto in Capricorn**: Transformation through discipline and authority. Pluto in Capricorn encourages restructuring traditional systems and achieving long-term goals.
- **Pluto in Aquarius**: Transformation through innovation and humanitarian efforts. Pluto in Aquarius promotes progressive change and collective empowerment.
- **Pluto in Pisces**: Transformation through spirituality and compassion. Pluto in Pisces fosters healing through empathy, creativity, and spiritual exploration.

- **Power and Rebirth**: Pluto's energy is associated with power dynamics, both personal and societal. It compels us to confront and transform areas of life where power and control issues arise. This process often involves facing our deepest fears and releasing what no longer serves us, leading to profound personal rebirth and empowerment.
- **Shadow Work and Psychological Depth**: Pluto governs the process of shadow work, where we explore and integrate the darker aspects of our psyche. This journey into the unconscious

mind helps us understand and heal deep-seated traumas and patterns. Pluto's influence can lead to significant psychological breakthroughs and emotional healing.

Hemp for Personal Transformation and Healing

Hemp, particularly products containing CBD, can support personal transformation and healing by promoting relaxation, reducing anxiety, and fostering a sense of inner peace. Here are some ways hemp can help you align with Pluto's transformative energy:

- **Promoting Relaxation and Calm**: CBD's anxiolytic properties can help reduce stress and anxiety, creating a calm and centered state of mind. This relaxation is essential for deep healing and transformative work.
- **Enhancing Meditation and Introspection**: Meditation is a powerful tool for transformation. CBD can enhance your meditation practice by promoting relaxation and focus. Incorporating CBD into your routine can help you reach a deeper state of mindfulness and connect with your inner self.
- **Supporting Emotional Balance**: Emotional stability is crucial for personal transformation. CBD can help regulate mood and promote emotional balance, allowing you to approach transformative work with a clear and open heart.
- **Improving Sleep Quality**: Adequate rest is essential for overall well-being and the ability to integrate transformative experiences. CBD can help improve sleep quality by promoting relaxation and reducing insomnia. A well-rested mind is more receptive to healing and change.
- **Alleviating Physical Discomfort**: Physical discomfort can hinder the process of transformation. CBD topicals, such as balms and creams, can help alleviate pain and inflammation, allowing you to stay focused and connected during deep healing practices.

Deep Healing Practices and Examples

To harness Pluto's energy for personal transformation and healing, incorporate the following deep healing practices into your routine:

Meditation and Introspection

- **CBD-Infused Deep Meditation**: Incorporate CBD oil into your meditation practice to enhance relaxation and focus. Take a few drops of CBD oil under your tongue before meditating. Find a quiet space, sit comfortably, and focus on your breath. Allow your mind to become quiet and receptive. Use this time to explore your inner world and connect with your deeper self.

- **Shadow Work Journaling**: Use a hemp journal to explore and integrate your shadow self. Write about your fears, insecurities, and unresolved emotions. Reflect on past experiences that still affect you and how you can release these burdens. The act of writing can help you process and integrate these aspects of yourself, leading to greater self-awareness and healing.

- **Guided Visualization**: Practice guided visualization to connect with Pluto's transformative energy. Use CBD to promote relaxation and enhance your visualization practice. Visualize yourself shedding old patterns and embracing new, empowered versions of yourself. Allow your intuition to guide you through the process of transformation.

Healing Rituals

- **Release and Let Go Ritual**: Create a ritual to release old patterns and negative energies. Write down what you want to let go of on a piece of paper. Use a hemp candle to safely burn the paper, visualizing the release of these burdens from your life. As the paper turns to ash, imagine yourself being freed from the past and open to new possibilities.

- **Transformative Bath Ritual**: Prepare a warm bath with a CBD-infused bath bomb to promote relaxation and healing. Add calming essential oils like lavender or eucalyptus. As you soak, visualize the water cleansing away negative energies and old patterns. Reflect on your journey and set intentions for your transformation. After your bath, write down any insights or intentions in your journal.
- **Crystal Healing**: Use crystals that resonate with Pluto's transformative energy, such as obsidian, amethyst, and black tourmaline. Incorporate these crystals into your meditation and healing practices. Use CBD-infused products to enhance relaxation and focus during your sessions. Hold the crystals or place them on your body, allowing their energy to support your transformation.

Therapeutic Practices

- **Energy Healing and Reiki**: Practice energy healing or Reiki to support your transformation and healing process. Use CBD to enhance relaxation and focus during your sessions. Pay attention to any intuitive impressions you receive while working with energy. Allow the healing energy to flow through you, releasing blockages and promoting balance.
- **Breathwork for Transformation**: Engage in breathwork exercises to release emotional and energetic blockages. Practice deep, intentional breathing to connect with your inner self and promote healing. Use CBD to promote relaxation and enhance your breathwork practice. Focus on your breath and allow yourself to release any tension or negative energy.
- **Holistic Therapies**: Explore holistic therapies such as acupuncture, massage, and aromatherapy to support your transformation. Use CBD topicals to enhance the benefits of these therapies. These practices can help balance your energy, release tension, and promote overall well-being.

Spiritual Practices

- **Connecting with Spirit Guides**: Practice connecting with your spirit guides or higher self for guidance and support during your transformation. Use CBD to promote relaxation and create a calm environment for your practice. Sit quietly, close your eyes, and invite your spirit guides to communicate with you. Pay attention to any intuitive impressions or messages you receive.
- **Chakra Balancing**: Work on balancing your chakras to support your transformation and healing. Use CBD-infused products to promote relaxation and support your chakra balancing practice. Visualize each chakra opening and aligning, allowing energy to flow freely through your body.
- **Rituals for Empowerment**: Create rituals that celebrate your transformation and empowerment. Light hemp-infused candles, use essential oils, and incorporate CBD into your rituals. Focus on embracing your new, empowered self and setting intentions for your future growth.

Personal Growth and Development

- **Setting Intentions and Goals**: Use a hemp journal to set intentions and goals for your personal transformation. Write down your aspirations and revisit them regularly to stay focused and motivated. Reflect on your progress and celebrate your achievements.
- **Positive Affirmations**: Practice positive affirmations to reinforce your sense of empowerment and growth. Write down affirmations like "I am strong and resilient" or "I embrace transformation and change." Repeat these affirmations daily to cultivate a positive mindset.
- **Building Resilience**: Focus on building resilience and emotional strength to support your transformation. Use CBD to manage

stress and maintain emotional balance. Engage in activities that promote resilience, such as physical exercise, mindfulness practices, and connecting with supportive friends and family.

In this chapter, we have explored the transformative power of Pluto, the benefits of using hemp for personal transformation and healing, and various deep healing practices to support your journey. By understanding Pluto's energy and incorporating hemp products into your routine, you can embrace profound personal growth, release old patterns, and achieve a sense of renewal and empowerment. As we continue our journey through this book, we will discover more ways to integrate hemp and astrology for holistic healing and personal growth.

Check out my Virtual dispensary for all your hemp needs: https://shift.store/sg1fan23477/retail

Chapter 20: Chiron - The Wounded Healer
Understanding Chiron's Role in Astrology

Chiron, known as the "Wounded Healer," is a celestial body that represents our deepest wounds and our capacity to heal others through our own healing journey. In mythology, Chiron was a wise centaur who, despite his own incurable wound, became a master healer and teacher. In astrology, Chiron's placement in the natal chart reveals where we carry our most profound pain and how we can transform that pain into wisdom and healing.

- **Astrological Significance**: Chiron's position in your natal chart highlights areas where you have experienced deep wounds, often from early life experiences. These wounds can manifest as physical, emotional, or psychological pain. Understanding Chiron's placement can provide insights into your healing journey and how you can use your experiences to help others.
  - **Chiron in Aries**: Wounds related to identity and self-expression. Healing through developing self-confidence and assertiveness.
  - **Chiron in Taurus**: Wounds related to self-worth and material security. Healing through finding inner value and stability.
  - **Chiron in Gemini**: Wounds related to communication and learning. Healing through finding your voice and embracing curiosity.
  - **Chiron in Cancer**: Wounds related to family and emotional security. Healing through nurturing self and others and creating a sense of belonging.

- **Chiron in Leo**: Wounds related to self-expression and recognition. Healing through embracing creativity and finding inner joy.
- **Chiron in Virgo**: Wounds related to perfectionism and service. Healing through accepting imperfection and finding balance in helping others.
- **Chiron in Libra**: Wounds related to relationships and balance. Healing through creating harmonious partnerships and self-love.
- **Chiron in Scorpio**: Wounds related to power and transformation. Healing through embracing change and finding empowerment.
- **Chiron in Sagittarius**: Wounds related to beliefs and freedom. Healing through expanding horizons and finding meaning.
- **Chiron in Capricorn**: Wounds related to authority and achievement. Healing through redefining success and finding personal integrity.
- **Chiron in Aquarius**: Wounds related to individuality and community. Healing through embracing uniqueness and contributing to the collective.
- **Chiron in Pisces**: Wounds related to spirituality and boundaries. Healing through developing faith and setting healthy limits.

- **Healing and Transformation**: Chiron's energy is transformative, encouraging us to face our deepest wounds and learn from them. This process involves vulnerability, self-compassion, and the willingness to embrace our pain as a source of strength. Through this journey, we can transform our wounds into wisdom and become healers for others.
- **The Wounded Healer Archetype**: The archetype of the wounded healer is central to Chiron's influence. It suggests that our own wounds can be a source of healing power when we

address and integrate them. By understanding and healing our own pain, we gain the empathy and insight needed to support others on their healing journeys.

Hemp for Healing Deep-Seated Wounds

Hemp, particularly products containing CBD, can support the healing of deep-seated wounds by promoting relaxation, reducing anxiety, and fostering a sense of inner peace. Here are some ways hemp can help you align with Chiron's healing energy:

- **Promoting Relaxation and Calm**: CBD's anxiolytic properties can help reduce stress and anxiety, creating a calm and centered state of mind. This relaxation is essential for deep healing and self-reflection.
- **Enhancing Emotional Balance**: Emotional stability is crucial for healing deep-seated wounds. CBD can help regulate mood and promote emotional balance, allowing you to approach your healing journey with a clear and open heart.
- **Supporting Meditation and Mindfulness**: Meditation is a powerful tool for healing. CBD can enhance your meditation practice by promoting relaxation and focus. Incorporating CBD into your routine can help you reach a deeper state of mindfulness and connect with your inner self.
- **Improving Sleep Quality**: Adequate rest is essential for overall well-being and the ability to integrate healing experiences. CBD can help improve sleep quality by promoting relaxation and reducing insomnia. A well-rested mind is more receptive to healing and transformation.
- **Alleviating Physical Discomfort**: Physical discomfort can hinder the healing process. CBD topicals, such as balms and creams, can help alleviate pain and inflammation, allowing you to stay focused and connected during your healing practices.

Personal Stories and Healing Journeys

To harness Chiron's energy for healing deep-seated wounds, incorporate the following practices and healing journeys into your routine:

Healing Practices

- **CBD-Infused Deep Meditation**: Incorporate CBD oil into your meditation practice to enhance relaxation and focus. Take a few drops of CBD oil under your tongue before meditating. Find a quiet space, sit comfortably, and focus on your breath. Allow your mind to become quiet and receptive. Use this time to explore your inner world and connect with your deeper self.

- **Shadow Work Journaling**: Use a hemp journal to explore and integrate your shadow self. Write about your fears, insecurities, and unresolved emotions. Reflect on past experiences that still affect you and how you can release these burdens. The act of writing can help you process and integrate these aspects of yourself, leading to greater self-awareness and healing.

- **Guided Visualization**: Practice guided visualization to connect with Chiron's healing energy. Use CBD to promote relaxation and enhance your visualization practice. Visualize yourself healing and transforming your wounds into sources of strength and wisdom. Allow your intuition to guide you through the process of healing.

Healing Rituals

- **Release and Let Go Ritual**: Create a ritual to release old wounds and negative energies. Write down what you want to let go of on a piece of paper. Use a hemp candle to safely burn the paper, visualizing the release of these burdens from your life. As the paper turns to ash, imagine yourself being freed from the past and open to new possibilities.

- **Transformative Bath Ritual**: Prepare a warm bath with a CBD-infused bath bomb to promote relaxation and healing. Add calming essential oils like lavender or eucalyptus. As you soak, visualize the water cleansing away negative energies and old wounds. Reflect on your journey and set intentions for your healing. After your bath, write down any insights or intentions in your journal.
- **Crystal Healing**: Use crystals that resonate with Chiron's healing energy, such as rose quartz, amethyst, and black obsidian. Incorporate these crystals into your meditation and healing practices. Use CBD-infused products to enhance relaxation and focus during your sessions. Hold the crystals or place them on your body, allowing their energy to support your healing.

Therapeutic Practices

- **Energy Healing and Reiki**: Practice energy healing or Reiki to support your healing journey. Use CBD to enhance relaxation and focus during your sessions. Pay attention to any intuitive impressions you receive while working with energy. Allow the healing energy to flow through you, releasing blockages and promoting balance.
- **Breathwork for Healing**: Engage in breathwork exercises to release emotional and energetic blockages. Practice deep, intentional breathing to connect with your inner self and promote healing. Use CBD to promote relaxation and enhance your breathwork practice. Focus on your breath and allow yourself to release any tension or negative energy.
- **Holistic Therapies**: Explore holistic therapies such as acupuncture, massage, and aromatherapy to support your healing journey. Use CBD topicals to enhance the benefits of these therapies. These practices can help balance your energy, release tension, and promote overall well-being.

Spiritual Practices

- **Connecting with Spirit Guides**: Practice connecting with your spirit guides or higher self for guidance and support during your healing journey. Use CBD to promote relaxation and create a calm environment for your practice. Sit quietly, close your eyes, and invite your spirit guides to communicate with you. Pay attention to any intuitive impressions or messages you receive.
- **Chakra Balancing**: Work on balancing your chakras to support your healing and transformation. Use CBD-infused products to promote relaxation and support your chakra balancing practice. Visualize each chakra opening and aligning, allowing energy to flow freely through your body.
- **Rituals for Empowerment**: Create rituals that celebrate your healing and empowerment. Light hemp-infused candles, use essential oils, and incorporate CBD into your rituals. Focus on embracing your healed self and setting intentions for your future growth.

Personal Growth and Development

- **Setting Intentions and Goals**: Use a hemp journal to set intentions and goals for your healing journey. Write down your aspirations and revisit them regularly to stay focused and motivated. Reflect on your progress and celebrate your achievements.
- **Positive Affirmations**: Practice positive affirmations to reinforce your sense of healing and growth. Write down affirmations like "I am whole and healed" or "I embrace my journey of transformation." Repeat these affirmations daily to cultivate a positive mindset.
- **Building Resilience**: Focus on building resilience and emotional strength to support your healing journey. Use CBD to manage stress and maintain emotional balance. Engage in activities that

promote resilience, such as physical exercise, mindfulness practices, and connecting with supportive friends and family.

In this chapter, we have explored Chiron's role in astrology, the benefits of using hemp for healing deep-seated wounds, and various healing practices and journeys to support your process. By understanding Chiron's energy and incorporating hemp products into your routine, you can embrace profound personal growth, transform your wounds into sources of strength, and achieve a sense of healing and empowerment. As we continue our journey through this book, we will discover more ways to integrate hemp and astrology for holistic healing and personal growth.

Check out my Virtual dispensary for all your hemp needs: https://shift.store/sg1fan23477/retail

Chapter 21: North and South Nodes
The Significance of the Lunar Nodes

In astrology, the lunar nodes are not planets but points where the Moon's orbit intersects the ecliptic plane. These points, known as the North Node (Rahu) and the South Node (Ketu), are significant because they reveal our soul's karmic journey and life purpose. The North Node represents our destiny, growth, and the lessons we need to learn, while the South Node symbolizes our past lives, inherent talents, and comfort zones.

- **North Node (Rahu)**: The North Node signifies the qualities, experiences, and life lessons that our soul needs to embrace in this lifetime. It points to our highest potential and the path we are meant to follow to achieve spiritual growth and fulfillment. The sign and house placement of the North Node in your natal chart indicate the areas where you need to step out of your comfort zone and pursue new experiences.
  - **North Node in Aries**: Embrace independence, courage, and leadership.
  - **North Node in Taurus**: Seek stability, self-worth, and material security.
  - **North Node in Gemini**: Focus on communication, learning, and adaptability.
  - **North Node in Cancer**: Nurture emotional connections and home life.
  - **North Node in Leo**: Express creativity, confidence, and self-love.
  - **North Node in Virgo**: Develop practicality, service, and attention to detail.

- **North Node in Libra**: Foster relationships, balance, and cooperation.
- **North Node in Scorpio**: Embrace transformation, power, and depth.
- **North Node in Sagittarius**: Pursue knowledge, freedom, and adventure.
- **North Node in Capricorn**: Seek discipline, ambition, and responsibility.
- **North Node in Aquarius**: Focus on innovation, individuality, and humanitarianism.
- **North Node in Pisces**: Embrace spirituality, compassion, and intuition.

- **South Node (Ketu)**: The South Node represents our past lives, karmic patterns, and the traits and skills we have already mastered. It symbolizes our comfort zone and the areas where we may feel a natural inclination but also where we need to release old habits and behaviors. The sign and house placement of the South Node in your natal chart indicate the areas where you may need to let go of past tendencies to achieve balance and growth.
  - **South Node in Aries**: Release selfishness, impulsiveness, and impatience.
  - **South Node in Taurus**: Let go of stubbornness, materialism, and possessiveness.
  - **South Node in Gemini**: Move beyond superficiality, gossip, and restlessness.
  - **South Node in Cancer**: Overcome dependency, insecurity, and clinginess.
  - **South Node in Leo**: Release arrogance, ego, and need for constant validation.
  - **South Node in Virgo**: Let go of perfectionism, criticism, and overanalysis.
  - **South Node in Libra**: Overcome indecision, people-pleasing, and codependency.

- ◦ **South Node in Scorpio**: Release obsession, secrecy, and control issues.
- ◦ **South Node in Sagittarius**: Move beyond dogmatism, recklessness, and restlessness.
- ◦ **South Node in Capricorn**: Overcome rigidity, workaholism, and detachment.
- ◦ **South Node in Aquarius**: Release detachment, rebellion, and unconventionality.
- ◦ **South Node in Pisces**: Let go of escapism, victim mentality, and confusion.
- **Balancing the Nodes**: The key to working with the lunar nodes is finding a balance between the qualities of the North and South Nodes. Embracing the lessons of the North Node while integrating the strengths of the South Node can lead to personal growth and fulfillment. The journey involves moving away from old patterns and embracing new opportunities for growth and transformation.

Hemp for Aligning with Life Purpose

Hemp, particularly products containing CBD, can support your journey in aligning with your life purpose by promoting relaxation, reducing anxiety, and fostering a sense of clarity and balance. Here are some ways hemp can help you align with the energy of the lunar nodes:

- **Promoting Relaxation and Calm**: CBD's anxiolytic properties can help reduce stress and anxiety, creating a calm and centered state of mind. This relaxation is essential for introspection and understanding your life purpose.
- **Enhancing Meditation and Mindfulness**: Meditation is a powerful tool for connecting with your life purpose. CBD can enhance your meditation practice by promoting relaxation and focus. Incorporating CBD into your routine can help you reach a deeper state of mindfulness and connect with your inner self.

- **Supporting Emotional Balance**: Emotional stability is crucial for understanding and aligning with your life purpose. CBD can help regulate mood and promote emotional balance, allowing you to approach your life journey with a clear and open heart.
- **Improving Sleep Quality**: Adequate rest is essential for overall well-being and the ability to integrate insights about your life purpose. CBD can help improve sleep quality by promoting relaxation and reducing insomnia. A well-rested mind is more receptive to guidance and inspiration.
- **Alleviating Physical Discomfort**: Physical discomfort can hinder the process of introspection and self-discovery. CBD topicals, such as balms and creams, can help alleviate pain and inflammation, allowing you to stay focused and connected during your reflective practices.

Practical Guidance and Exercises

To harness the energy of the lunar nodes for aligning with your life purpose, incorporate the following practical guidance and exercises into your routine:

Meditation and Introspection

- **CBD-Infused Meditation**: Incorporate CBD oil into your meditation practice to enhance relaxation and focus. Take a few drops of CBD oil under your tongue before meditating. Find a quiet space, sit comfortably, and focus on your breath. Allow your mind to become quiet and receptive. Use this time to explore your inner world and connect with your life purpose.
- **Node Reflection Meditation**: Practice meditation specifically focused on the lunar nodes. Visualize the qualities and lessons of your North Node and the strengths and habits of your South Node. Reflect on how you can balance these energies in your life. Use CBD to enhance relaxation and deepen your introspection.

Journaling and Self-Reflection

- **Life Purpose Journaling**: Use a hemp journal to explore your life purpose and the lessons of your lunar nodes. Write about your aspirations, strengths, and areas where you feel challenged. Reflect on how the qualities of your North Node can guide you toward your purpose and how the strengths of your South Node can support you.
- **Goal Setting and Tracking**: Set specific goals aligned with your life purpose and the lessons of your North Node. Use CBD to promote relaxation and clarity while setting your intentions. Regularly review and track your progress in your journal, adjusting your goals as needed.

Practical Exercises

- **Balancing Activities**: Engage in activities that balance the qualities of your North and South Nodes. For example, if your North Node is in Taurus and your South Node is in Scorpio, focus on grounding activities like gardening or cooking, while also exploring transformative practices like deep meditation or emotional healing.
- **Mindful Action**: Practice mindful action by consciously incorporating the lessons of your North Node into your daily life. Use CBD to stay calm and focused as you embrace new experiences and step out of your comfort zone. Reflect on your actions and their alignment with your life purpose.

Spiritual Practices

- **Connecting with Higher Self**: Practice connecting with your higher self for guidance on your life purpose. Use CBD to promote relaxation and create a calm environment for your practice.

Sit quietly, close your eyes, and invite your higher self to communicate with you. Pay attention to any intuitive impressions or messages you receive.

- **Chakra Balancing**: Work on balancing your chakras to support your alignment with your life purpose. Use CBD-infused products to promote relaxation and support your chakra balancing practice. Visualize each chakra opening and aligning, allowing energy to flow freely through your body.

Personal Growth and Development

- **Setting Intentions and Goals**: Use a hemp journal to set intentions and goals for aligning with your life purpose. Write down your aspirations and revisit them regularly to stay focused and motivated. Reflect on your progress and celebrate your achievements.
- **Positive Affirmations**: Practice positive affirmations to reinforce your alignment with your life purpose. Write down affirmations like "I am aligned with my highest purpose" or "I embrace the lessons of my North Node." Repeat these affirmations daily to cultivate a positive mindset.
- **Building Resilience**: Focus on building resilience and emotional strength to support your journey towards your life purpose. Use CBD to manage stress and maintain emotional balance. Engage in activities that promote resilience, such as physical exercise, mindfulness practices, and connecting with supportive friends and family.

Creative Practices

- **Vision Boarding**: Create a vision board that reflects your life purpose and the lessons of your North Node. Use images, quotes, and symbols that resonate with your aspirations and goals. Place your vision board in a prominent location as a daily reminder of your path.

- **Artistic Expression**: Engage in artistic activities like painting, drawing, or music to express your journey towards your life purpose. Use CBD to reduce anxiety and enhance your creative flow. Allow your intuition to guide your artistic expression, and pay attention to any insights or messages that emerge through your art.
- **Creative Visualization**: Use creative visualization to align with your life purpose and manifest your goals. Use CBD to promote relaxation and clarity during your visualization practice. Close your eyes, visualize your goals and desires in detail, and feel the emotions associated with achieving them. This practice can help you tap into your intuition and align with your higher self.

Holistic Therapies

- **Energy Healing and Reiki**: Practice energy healing or Reiki to support your alignment with your life purpose. Use CBD to enhance relaxation and focus during your sessions. Pay attention to any intuitive impressions you receive while working with energy. Allow the healing energy to flow through you, releasing blockages and promoting balance.
- **Holistic Therapies**: Explore holistic therapies such as acupuncture, massage, and aromatherapy to support your journey. Use CBD topicals to enhance the benefits of these therapies. These practices can help balance your energy, release tension, and promote overall well-being.
- **Breathwork for Clarity**: Engage in breathwork exercises to clear your mind and connect with your life purpose. Practice deep, intentional breathing to release any tension and promote mental clarity. Use CBD to enhance relaxation and focus during your breathwork practice.

Connecting with Nature

- **Nature Meditation**: Spend time in nature to connect with the energy of the Earth and align with your life purpose. Use CBD-infused products to promote relaxation and mindfulness during your nature meditation. Sit quietly in a natural setting, observe your surroundings, and allow yourself to become attuned to the energies of nature.
- **Grounding Practices**: Practice grounding techniques to stay connected to the Earth's energy and enhance your alignment with your life purpose. Walk barefoot on grass or sand, spend time in a garden, or use grounding crystals like hematite or smoky quartz. Incorporate CBD into your grounding practices to enhance relaxation and focus.

Community and Support

- **Building Connections**: Foster connections with like-minded individuals who share your interests and values. Join clubs, attend events, or participate in online communities to build supportive relationships and expand your social network.
- **Mentorship and Guidance**: Seek mentorship or guidance from individuals who inspire you and align with your life purpose. Use CBD to manage stress and maintain emotional balance while seeking and receiving guidance. Reflect on the advice and insights you receive, and incorporate them into your journey.
- **Volunteering and Service**: Engage in volunteer work or community service aligned with your life purpose and the lessons of your North Node. Use CBD to manage stress and maintain emotional balance while serving others. Reflect on your experiences and the impact of your contributions on your personal growth.

Practical Applications

- **Daily Reflection**: Set aside time each day for reflection on your life purpose and the lessons of your lunar nodes. Use a hemp journal to write about your experiences, insights, and progress. Reflect on how you can incorporate these lessons into your daily life and actions.
- **Action Steps**: Identify specific action steps that align with your life purpose and the lessons of your North Node. Create a plan to integrate these steps into your routine, and use CBD to maintain focus and motivation. Regularly review and adjust your plan as needed to stay on track.
- **Gratitude Practice**: Cultivate a gratitude practice to reinforce your alignment with your life purpose. Use a hemp journal to write down things you are grateful for each day. Reflect on how these blessings support your journey and the lessons of your lunar nodes.

In this chapter, we have explored the significance of the lunar nodes, the benefits of using hemp for aligning with your life purpose, and various practical guidance and exercises to support your journey. By understanding the energy of the lunar nodes and incorporating hemp products into your routine, you can embrace your highest potential, balance past patterns with new growth, and achieve a sense of fulfillment and purpose. As we continue our journey through this book, we will discover more ways to integrate hemp and astrology for holistic healing and personal growth.

Check out my Virtual dispensary for all your hemp needs: https://shift.store/sg1fan23477/retail

Chapter 22: Planetary Retrogrades
The Impact of Retrogrades in Astrology

Retrogrades are periods when a planet appears to move backward in its orbit from our perspective on Earth. This optical illusion is caused by the relative positions and motions of the Earth and the other planets. Retrogrades are significant in astrology because they represent times of introspection, review, and reassessment. Each planet's retrograde has a unique influence on various aspects of life.

- **Mercury Retrograde**: Occurs three to four times a year for about three weeks. Mercury retrograde is infamous for causing communication breakdowns, technological glitches, travel delays, and misunderstandings. It's a time to revisit old projects, clarify communication, and double-check details.
- **Venus Retrograde**: Happens approximately every 18 months for about six weeks. During Venus retrograde, issues related to love, relationships, beauty, and finances come to the forefront. It's a period for reevaluating relationships, reassessing values, and reflecting on personal worth.
- **Mars Retrograde**: Occurs about every two years for approximately two and a half months. Mars retrograde affects energy

levels, motivation, and assertiveness. It's a time to reconsider actions, review strategies, and resolve internal conflicts.

- **Jupiter Retrograde**: Happens once a year for about four months. During Jupiter retrograde, growth, expansion, and belief systems are examined. It's a time for introspection, philosophical reflection, and revisiting long-term goals.
- **Saturn Retrograde**: Occurs annually for about four and a half months. Saturn retrograde is a period for reviewing responsibilities, structures, and boundaries. It's a time to reassess commitments, refine plans, and address unfinished business.
- **Uranus Retrograde**: Happens once a year for about five months. Uranus retrograde prompts reevaluation of innovation, rebellion, and personal freedom. It's a period for internal change, breaking free from outdated patterns, and exploring new perspectives.
- **Neptune Retrograde**: Occurs annually for about five months. Neptune retrograde is a time for introspection, spiritual growth, and confronting illusions. It's a period to deepen spiritual practices, clarify dreams, and release escapism.
- **Pluto Retrograde**: Happens once a year for about five to six months. Pluto retrograde is a time for deep psychological transformation, confronting power dynamics, and releasing old traumas. It's a period for profound inner work and rebirth.
- **Chiron Retrograde**: Occurs once a year for about five months. Chiron retrograde is a period for healing deep-seated wounds, addressing past pain, and gaining wisdom through inner reflection.

Coping with Retrogrades Using Hemp

Hemp, particularly products containing CBD, can support you during retrograde periods by promoting relaxation, reducing anxiety, and fostering a sense of balance and clarity. Here are some ways hemp can help you cope with the challenges and opportunities of retrogrades:

- **Promoting Relaxation and Calm**: CBD's anxiolytic properties can help reduce stress and anxiety, creating a calm and centered state of mind. This relaxation is essential during retrogrades, when tensions can run high and patience is tested.

- **Enhancing Focus and Clarity**: Retrogrades often require careful review and reassessment. CBD can improve mental clarity and focus, helping you navigate through the confusion and introspection that retrogrades bring.

- **Supporting Emotional Balance**: Emotional stability is crucial during retrogrades, especially when dealing with relationships and personal growth. CBD can help regulate mood and promote emotional balance, allowing you to approach retrograde challenges with a clear and open heart.

- **Improving Sleep Quality**: Adequate rest is essential for overall well-being and the ability to integrate retrograde experiences. CBD can help improve sleep quality by promoting relaxation and reducing insomnia. A well-rested mind is more resilient and better equipped to handle the introspective work required during retrogrades.

- **Alleviating Physical Discomfort**: Physical discomfort can be exacerbated during retrogrades, adding to the overall stress. CBD topicals, such as balms and creams, can help alleviate pain and inflammation, allowing you to stay focused and connected during your reflective practices.

Rituals and Reflective Practices

To harness the energy of retrogrades for personal growth and transformation, incorporate the following rituals and reflective practices into your routine:

Mercury Retrograde Rituals

- **Communication Cleansing**: Use CBD oil to promote relaxation before engaging in a communication cleansing ritual. Light a hemp-infused candle and write down any misunderstandings or unresolved conversations. Burn the paper safely, visualizing the release of negative communication patterns. Use this time to clarify your thoughts and intentions.

- **Digital Detox**: During Mercury retrograde, take a break from excessive screen time and digital distractions. Use CBD to enhance relaxation and focus on mindful activities like reading, journaling, or spending time in nature. Reflect on how technology impacts your life and set intentions for healthier digital habits.

Venus Retrograde Rituals

- **Self-Love Ritual**: Create a self-love ritual using CBD-infused bath bombs or oils. Draw a warm bath, add calming essential oils like rose or lavender, and soak while reflecting on your self-worth and values. Use this time to nurture yourself and reaffirm your commitment to self-love and self-care.

- **Relationship Reflection**: Use CBD to promote relaxation before engaging in a relationship reflection exercise. Write down the qualities you value in relationships and any patterns you wish to change. Reflect on past relationships and identify lessons learned. Set intentions for healthier and more fulfilling connections.

Mars Retrograde Rituals

- **Energy Reassessment**: During Mars retrograde, reassess how you use your energy and assertiveness. Use CBD to enhance focus and relaxation. Create a plan for channeling your energy more effectively, whether through physical activity, creative projects, or strategic planning. Reflect on how you can balance action with reflection.

- **Conflict Resolution**: Use CBD to promote calm before addressing any unresolved conflicts. Write down the issues and your desired outcomes. Engage in open and honest communication, focusing on finding mutually beneficial solutions. Reflect on how you can approach conflicts with more patience and understanding.

Jupiter Retrograde Rituals

- **Philosophical Reflection**: Use CBD to enhance relaxation and clarity during philosophical reflection. Spend time reading or writing about your beliefs, values, and long-term goals. Reflect on how these have evolved and set intentions for further personal and spiritual growth.
- **Vision Quest**: During Jupiter retrograde, embark on a personal vision quest. Use CBD-infused products to promote relaxation and mindfulness. Spend time in nature, meditate, and seek inner guidance. Reflect on your life's purpose and the steps you need to take to align with it.

Saturn Retrograde Rituals

- **Responsibility Review**: Use CBD to promote relaxation before engaging in a responsibility review. Write down your commitments and assess their alignment with your goals and values. Reflect on any areas where you need to set boundaries or restructure responsibilities.
- **Legacy Planning**: During Saturn retrograde, reflect on the legacy you wish to leave. Use CBD to enhance focus and clarity. Write down your long-term goals and the steps needed to achieve them. Reflect on how you can build a lasting impact through discipline and dedication.

Uranus Retrograde Rituals

- **Innovation Journal**: Use CBD to promote relaxation and creativity before journaling about innovative ideas and personal freedom. Write down any unconventional thoughts and reflect on how you can integrate them into your life. Set intentions for embracing change and breaking free from outdated patterns.
- **Rebellion Ritual**: During Uranus retrograde, perform a rebellion ritual. Use CBD-infused products to promote relaxation and focus. Write down any societal or personal norms you wish to challenge. Burn the paper safely, visualizing the release of restrictive patterns. Reflect on how you can embrace your individuality and foster positive change.

Neptune Retrograde Rituals

- **Dream Journal**: Use CBD to enhance relaxation and dream recall. Keep a hemp journal by your bedside and write down your dreams upon waking. Reflect on the symbols and messages within your dreams. Use this time to deepen your spiritual practices and connect with your subconscious mind.
- **Illusion Release**: During Neptune retrograde, focus on releasing illusions and gaining clarity. Use CBD to promote relaxation before engaging in a guided visualization. Visualize a fog lifting from your mind, revealing clear and truthful insights. Reflect on any areas of your life where you need to seek greater honesty and authenticity.

Pluto Retrograde Rituals

- **Shadow Work**: Use CBD to promote relaxation and emotional balance before engaging in shadow work. Write about your fears, insecurities, and unresolved traumas. Reflect on how these have shaped your life and set intentions for healing and transformation.

- **Transformation Ritual**: During Pluto retrograde, create a transformation ritual. Use CBD-infused products to enhance relaxation and focus. Write down any patterns or behaviors you wish to release. Burn the paper safely, visualizing the shedding of old skins and the emergence of a new, empowered self.

Chiron Retrograde Rituals

- **Healing Journal**: Use CBD to promote relaxation and introspection before journaling about your deepest wounds and healing journey. Reflect on past pain and the wisdom gained from it. Set intentions for continued healing and growth.
- **Healing Ritual**: During Chiron retrograde, perform a healing ritual. Use CBD-infused products to promote relaxation and emotional balance. Light candles, use healing crystals, and create a sacred space. Reflect on your healing journey and invite in the energy of compassion and self-acceptance.

General Reflective Practices for Retrogrades

- **Meditation and Mindfulness**: Practice meditation and mindfulness regularly during retrogrades. Use CBD to enhance relaxation and focus. Set aside time each day to reflect on the themes of the retrograde and how they apply to your life.
- **Gratitude Practice**: Cultivate a gratitude practice to maintain a positive mindset during retrogrades. Use a hemp journal to write down things you are grateful for each day. Reflect on how these blessings support your personal growth and resilience.
- **Energy Clearing**: Regularly clear your energy using techniques like smudging, sound healing, or Reiki. Use CBD to promote relaxation and create a calm environment for your energy clearing practices. Reflect on any stagnant or negative energies you need to release.

In this chapter, we have explored the impact of retrogrades in astrology, the benefits of using hemp to cope with retrograde challenges, and various rituals and reflective practices to support your journey. By understanding the energy of retrogrades and incorporating hemp products into your routine, you can navigate these periods with grace, embrace introspection, and achieve personal growth and transformation. As we continue our journey through this book, we will discover more ways to integrate hemp and astrology for holistic healing and personal growth.

Check out my Virtual dispensary for all your hemp needs: https://shift.store/sg1fan23477/retail

Chapter 23: The Great Conjunctions
Understanding Conjunctions of Jupiter and Saturn

Great Conjunctions occur when Jupiter and Saturn align in the same sign of the zodiac, an event that happens approximately every 20 years. These conjunctions are significant in astrology because they symbolize major shifts in societal structures, collective consciousness, and long-term trends. The combination of Jupiter's expansive and optimistic energy with Saturn's disciplined and structured influence creates a powerful dynamic that can lead to profound changes.

- **Astrological Significance**: The Great Conjunction represents a merging of opposites, balancing growth and expansion (Jupiter) with restriction and discipline (Saturn). This alignment marks the beginning of new cycles, influencing economic, political, and cultural shifts. Understanding the energy of the Great Conjunction can help us navigate these changes and align with the collective evolution.
  - **Jupiter**: Associated with growth, abundance, optimism, and higher learning. Jupiter's influence encourages expansion, exploration, and the pursuit of wisdom and truth.
  - **Saturn**: Represents structure, discipline, responsibility, and boundaries. Saturn's energy emphasizes realism, hard work, and long-term planning.
- **Themes of Great Conjunctions**: Each Great Conjunction occurs in a different zodiac sign, influencing the themes and areas of life affected by this powerful alignment. The sign in which the conjunction occurs sets the tone for the next 20-year cycle.
  - **Conjunction in Earth Signs (Taurus, Virgo, Capricorn):** Focus on material resources, stability, environmental sustainability, and practical innovations.

- ◦ **Conjunction in Air Signs (Gemini, Libra, Aquarius):** Emphasis on communication, technology, social structures, and intellectual advancements.
  - ◦ **Conjunction in Water Signs (Cancer, Scorpio, Pisces):** Themes of emotional transformation, spirituality, healing, and deep psychological changes.
  - ◦ **Conjunction in Fire Signs (Aries, Leo, Sagittarius):** Focus on leadership, creativity, personal freedom, and dynamic transformations.
- **Cycle of Conjunctions:** The Great Conjunctions follow a pattern, occurring in signs of the same element for approximately 200 years before shifting to the next element. This cycle influences long-term societal trends and the collective evolution of humanity.

Harnessing Their Power with Hemp

Hemp, particularly products containing CBD, can support you in harnessing the power of Great Conjunctions by promoting relaxation, reducing anxiety, and fostering a sense of clarity and balance. Here are some ways hemp can help you align with the transformative energy of Jupiter and Saturn:

- **Promoting Relaxation and Calm:** CBD's anxiolytic properties can help reduce stress and anxiety, creating a calm and centered state of mind. This relaxation is essential for navigating the intense energy of Great Conjunctions and integrating their transformative potential.
- **Enhancing Focus and Clarity:** The energy of Great Conjunctions often requires careful planning and disciplined action. CBD can improve mental clarity and focus, helping you stay organized and aligned with your long-term goals.
- **Supporting Emotional Balance:** Emotional stability is crucial during periods of major transformation. CBD can help regulate

mood and promote emotional balance, allowing you to approach changes with a clear and open heart.

- **Improving Sleep Quality**: Adequate rest is essential for overall well-being and the ability to integrate the powerful energies of Great Conjunctions. CBD can help improve sleep quality by promoting relaxation and reducing insomnia. A well-rested mind is more resilient and better equipped to handle transformative shifts.

- **Alleviating Physical Discomfort**: Physical discomfort can be exacerbated during times of significant change, adding to overall stress. CBD topicals, such as balms and creams, can help alleviate pain and inflammation, allowing you to stay focused and connected during your reflective practices.

Historical Significance and Modern Applications

Great Conjunctions have played significant roles in shaping historical events and societal trends. Understanding their historical significance and applying their lessons to modern life can help us navigate current and future changes effectively.

Historical Significance

- **Medieval and Renaissance Eras**: Great Conjunctions were seen as omens of significant events, such as the rise and fall of empires, the birth of great leaders, and major religious transformations. Astrologers of these times used conjunctions to predict political and social changes.

- **Industrial Revolution**: The Great Conjunctions in Earth signs during the 19th century coincided with the Industrial Revolution, marking significant advancements in technology, industry, and economic structures. These conjunctions emphasized material growth, innovation, and the establishment of new societal frameworks.

- **Technological Age**: The shift to Air sign conjunctions in the late 20th and early 21st centuries has coincided with the rise of the information age, technological advancements, and changes in communication and social structures. The conjunction in Aquarius in 2020, for example, marked a significant shift towards innovation, digital transformation, and collective consciousness.

Modern Applications

- **Navigating Economic Shifts**: Great Conjunctions often coincide with significant economic changes. Use CBD to maintain emotional balance and mental clarity while navigating these shifts. Reflect on how you can adapt to new economic trends and align your financial goals with the evolving landscape.
- **Embracing Technological Advancements**: The energy of Great Conjunctions in Air signs emphasizes technological innovation and intellectual advancements. Use CBD to enhance focus and clarity while exploring new technologies and learning new skills. Stay open to new ideas and embrace the opportunities for growth and expansion.
- **Fostering Social Change**: Great Conjunctions often signal shifts in social structures and collective consciousness. Use CBD to promote relaxation and emotional balance while engaging in social activism and community building. Reflect on how you can contribute to positive social change and align your actions with the greater good.
- **Personal Transformation and Growth**: The energy of Great Conjunctions can be harnessed for personal transformation and growth. Use CBD to support your introspective practices and set long-term goals aligned with your highest potential. Reflect on how you can integrate the lessons of Jupiter and Saturn into your personal and spiritual development.

Practical Exercises

- **Vision Boarding for Long-Term Goals**: Create a vision board that reflects your long-term goals and aspirations. Use images, quotes, and symbols that resonate with the themes of the current Great Conjunction. Place your vision board in a prominent location as a daily reminder of your path. Use CBD to promote relaxation and clarity while creating your vision board.
- **Reflective Journaling**: Use a hemp journal to reflect on the themes of the current Great Conjunction and how they apply to your life. Write about your goals, aspirations, and the steps you need to take to achieve them. Use CBD to enhance focus and clarity while journaling.
- **Meditation and Visualization**: Practice meditation and visualization to connect with the energy of the Great Conjunction. Use CBD to promote relaxation and deepen your meditation practice. Visualize yourself aligning with the transformative energy of Jupiter and Saturn and integrating their lessons into your life.
- **Astrological Planning**: Use astrology to plan your actions and set goals aligned with the energy of the Great Conjunction. Use CBD to enhance focus and clarity while studying astrological charts and planning your activities. Reflect on how you can harness the energy of the conjunction to achieve your long-term aspirations.
- **Community Engagement**: Engage with your community to harness the collective energy of the Great Conjunction. Use CBD to maintain emotional balance and promote positive interactions. Participate in community events, social activism, and collaborative projects that align with the themes of the conjunction.

Rituals for Harnessing Great Conjunction Energy

- **New Moon Intention Setting**: Align your intention-setting rituals with the cycles of the Moon and the energy of the Great Conjunction. Use CBD to enhance relaxation and focus during your rituals. Write down your intentions for growth and transformation and visualize their manifestation.
- **Seasonal Reflection**: Reflect on the changing seasons and how they align with the themes of the Great Conjunction. Use CBD to promote relaxation and clarity during your reflections. Set goals and intentions for each season, aligning your actions with the natural cycles and the energy of the conjunction.
- **Energy Clearing**: Regularly clear your energy using techniques like smudging, sound healing, or Reiki. Use CBD to promote relaxation and create a calm environment for your energy clearing practices. Reflect on any stagnant or negative energies you need to release to align with the transformative energy of the Great Conjunction.

In this chapter, we have explored the significance of Great Conjunctions of Jupiter and Saturn, the benefits of using hemp to harness their power, and their historical significance and modern applications. By understanding the energy of Great Conjunctions and incorporating hemp products into your routine, you can navigate these powerful alignments with grace, embrace transformation, and achieve personal and collective growth. As we continue our journey through this book, we will discover more ways to integrate hemp and astrology for holistic healing and personal growth.

Check out my Virtual dispensary for all your hemp needs: https://shift.store/sg1fan23477/retail

Chapter 24: Celestial Events and Celebrations
Major Celestial Events: Solstices, Equinoxes, and Meteor Showers
Celestial events such as solstices, equinoxes, and meteor showers have been celebrated throughout human history for their profound impact on our connection to nature and the cosmos. These events mark significant points in the Earth's journey around the Sun and offer opportunities for reflection, celebration, and alignment with natural rhythms.

- **Solstices**: The solstices occur twice a year, marking the longest and shortest days. The Summer Solstice, around June 21, is the longest day of the year and signifies the height of summer. The Winter Solstice, around December 21, is the shortest day of the year and marks the beginning of winter. Solstices are times of celebration, renewal, and reflection on the cycles of light and darkness.

- **Equinoxes**: Equinoxes occur twice a year, around March 21 and September 21, when day and night are of equal length. The Spring Equinox, or Vernal Equinox, marks the beginning of spring and symbolizes rebirth and new beginnings. The Fall Equinox, or Autumnal Equinox, signals the start of autumn and is a time of harvest and gratitude. Equinoxes are moments of balance and transition.

- **Meteor Showers**: Meteor showers occur when the Earth passes through the debris left by comets. Notable meteor showers include the Perseids in August and the Geminids in December. These events are opportunities for awe and wonder, connecting us to the vastness of the cosmos and the beauty of fleeting moments.

Celebrating with Hemp Rituals and Ceremonies

Hemp, particularly products containing CBD, can enhance your celebrations of celestial events by promoting relaxation, mindfulness, and a deeper connection to the natural world. Here are some ways to incorporate hemp into your rituals and ceremonies:

Solstice Celebrations

- **Summer Solstice Ritual**: Celebrate the Summer Solstice with a CBD-infused picnic or outdoor gathering. Use CBD oil or edibles to promote relaxation and enjoyment. Create a ritual of gratitude for the abundance of light and growth. Light candles or a bonfire to symbolize the Sun's energy and reflect on your personal growth and achievements.

- **Winter Solstice Ceremony**: Honor the Winter Solstice with a reflective ceremony. Use CBD-infused tea or hot cocoa to create a warm and calming atmosphere. Light candles or a Yule log to symbolize the return of the light. Reflect on the past year, release what no longer serves you, and set intentions for the coming year.

Equinox Celebrations

- **Spring Equinox Ritual**: Celebrate the Spring Equinox with a renewal ritual. Use CBD-infused products to promote relaxation and clarity. Plant seeds or flowers to symbolize new beginnings and growth. Reflect on your goals and set intentions for the new season. Use this time to cleanse your space, physically and energetically.

- **Fall Equinox Ceremony**: Honor the Fall Equinox with a gratitude ceremony. Use CBD to enhance relaxation and mindfulness. Create a harvest altar with seasonal fruits, vegetables, and flowers. Reflect on the abundance in your life and express gratitude for your blessings. Share a meal with loved ones and celebrate the harvest.

Meteor Shower Observations

- **Night Sky Meditation**: During a meteor shower, find a quiet outdoor space to observe the night sky. Use CBD to promote relaxation and deepen your connection to the cosmos. Lay on a blanket, look up at the stars, and practice mindful breathing. Reflect on your place in the universe and the beauty of fleeting moments.
- **Wishing Ceremony**: Create a wishing ceremony during a meteor shower. Use CBD-infused products to promote calm and focus. Write down your wishes or intentions on small pieces of paper. As you see meteors, visualize your wishes being carried into the universe. Burn the papers safely, releasing your intentions into the cosmos.

Community Practices and Global Traditions

Celestial events are celebrated in diverse ways across cultures and communities, highlighting our shared connection to the cosmos. Here are some examples of community practices and global traditions:

Community Practices

- **Public Solstice Celebrations**: Many communities host public celebrations for the solstices, including festivals, parades, and gatherings. These events often feature music, dance, food, and communal rituals. Participating in these celebrations can foster a sense of community and connection to the natural world.
- **Equinox Festivals**: Equinox festivals often include activities like outdoor markets, art exhibits, and cultural performances. These events celebrate the balance of light and dark and the changing seasons. Community members come together to share their talents, support local artisans, and enjoy the beauty of nature.
- **Astronomy Nights**: Local astronomy clubs and organizations often host events during meteor showers and other celestial

occurrences. These events may include stargazing sessions, telescope viewings, and educational talks. Participating in astronomy nights can deepen your appreciation for the cosmos and connect you with fellow sky enthusiasts.

Global Traditions

- **Stonehenge Solstice Celebrations (England):** Stonehenge is a famous site for solstice celebrations, where people gather to witness the sunrise or sunset aligning with the ancient stones. These gatherings include drumming, chanting, and communal rituals, celebrating the cycles of nature.
- **Inti Raymi (Peru):** Inti Raymi, the Festival of the Sun, is an ancient Incan celebration of the Winter Solstice. Held in Cusco, Peru, this festival includes traditional music, dance, and rituals honoring the Sun God Inti. Participants celebrate the return of the Sun and the renewal of life.
- **Nowruz (Iran and Central Asia):** Nowruz, the Persian New Year, is celebrated on the Spring Equinox. This festival marks the beginning of spring and includes rituals such as cleaning homes, visiting friends and family, and preparing symbolic foods. Nowruz celebrates renewal, hope, and the victory of light over darkness.
- **Chuseok (Korea):** Chuseok, also known as Korean Thanksgiving, is celebrated around the Fall Equinox. This harvest festival includes ancestral rituals, family gatherings, and traditional foods. Chuseok honors the ancestors and celebrates the abundance of the harvest.
- **Lunar New Year (East Asia):** The Lunar New Year is celebrated in many East Asian cultures, marking the beginning of the lunar calendar. Festivities include dragon dances, fireworks, family reunions, and symbolic foods. This celebration emphasizes renewal, prosperity, and the harmony of the cosmos.

Incorporating Global Traditions into Personal Practice

- **Creating a Solstice Altar**: Draw inspiration from global traditions to create a solstice altar. Include elements such as candles, seasonal plants, crystals, and symbols of the Sun. Use CBD-infused products to enhance relaxation and focus during your altar rituals. Reflect on the universal themes of renewal, light, and transformation.

- **Participating in Community Events**: Join local community events that celebrate celestial occurrences. Use CBD to promote relaxation and openness, allowing you to fully engage with the celebrations. Participate in communal rituals, share your experiences, and connect with others who share your appreciation for the cosmos.

- **Learning About Cultural Practices**: Educate yourself about how different cultures celebrate celestial events. Incorporate elements of these traditions into your personal practices, respecting their cultural significance. Use CBD to enhance relaxation and mindfulness as you explore new rituals and ceremonies

Integrating Celestial Celebrations into Daily Life

Incorporating the energy of celestial events into your daily life can enhance your connection to the cosmos and promote personal growth. Here are some tips for integrating these celebrations into your routine:

Daily Reflection

- **Morning Intention Setting**: Start your day by setting intentions aligned with the current celestial energy. Use CBD to promote relaxation and clarity. Reflect on your goals and how you can align your actions with the natural rhythms of the cosmos.

- **Evening Gratitude Practice**: End your day with a gratitude practice, reflecting on the blessings and lessons of the day. Use CBD to enhance relaxation and mindfulness. Write down things you are grateful for and reflect on how you can carry this gratitude into your celestial celebrations.

Mindful Movement

- **Yoga and Tai Chi**: Incorporate mindful movement practices like yoga or Tai Chi into your routine. Use CBD to promote relaxation and enhance your connection to your body and breath. Align your practice with the themes of celestial events, focusing on balance, renewal, and transformation.
- **Nature Walks**: Spend time in nature to connect with the energy of celestial events. Use CBD-infused products to enhance relaxation and mindfulness during your walks. Reflect on the changing seasons and the cycles of nature as you walk.

Creative Expression

- **Artistic Rituals**: Use artistic expression as a form of celebration and reflection. Create paintings, drawings, or crafts inspired by celestial events. Use CBD to reduce anxiety and enhance your creative flow. Allow your intuition to guide your artistic process and reflect on the themes of renewal and transformation.
- **Music and Dance**: Incorporate music and dance into your celebrations. Use CBD to promote relaxation and openness. Create playlists or choreograph dances inspired by celestial events. Use music and movement to express your connection to the cosmos and the natural world.

Spiritual Practices

- **Meditation and Visualization**: Practice meditation and visualization to connect with the energy of celestial events. Use CBD to enhance relaxation and deepen your meditation practice.

Visualize yourself aligning with the natural rhythms and integrating the lessons of the cosmos.

- **Chakra Balancing**: Work on balancing your chakras to align with the energy of celestial events. Use CBD-infused products to promote relaxation and support your chakra balancing practice. Visualize each chakra opening and aligning, allowing energy to flow freely through your body.

Community Engagement

- **Hosting Gatherings**: Host gatherings with friends and family to celebrate celestial events. Use CBD to promote relaxation and create a welcoming atmosphere. Share rituals, meals, and reflections with your loved ones, fostering a sense of community and connection.
- **Volunteering and Service**: Engage in volunteer work or community service aligned with the themes of celestial events. Use CBD to manage stress and maintain emotional balance while serving others. Reflect on how your actions contribute to the greater good and the harmony of the cosmos.

In this chapter, we have explored major celestial events such as solstices, equinoxes, and meteor showers, the benefits of celebrating with hemp rituals and ceremonies, and various community practices and global traditions. By understanding the energy of these celestial events and incorporating hemp products into your celebrations, you can deepen your connection to the cosmos, embrace natural rhythms, and achieve personal and collective growth. As we continue our journey through this book, we will discover more ways to integrate hemp and astrology for holistic healing and personal development.

Check out my Virtual dispensary for all your hemp needs: https://shift.store/sg1fan23477/retail

Chapter 25: Aries: The Pioneer Spirit
Characteristics and Traits of Aries

Aries, the first sign of the zodiac, is known for its dynamic and pioneering spirit. Ruled by Mars, the planet of action and desire, Aries embodies energy, enthusiasm, and a drive to lead and innovate. This cardinal fire sign marks the beginning of the astrological year and represents new beginnings, courage, and the will to forge ahead.

- **Positive Traits:**
  - **Courageous**: Aries individuals are fearless and willing to take risks. They are often the first to try new things and lead others into uncharted territory.
  - **Energetic**: With boundless energy, Aries people are always on the go. They have a zest for life and are constantly seeking new adventures and challenges.
  - **Confident**: Aries exudes confidence and self-assurance. They believe in their abilities and are not afraid to assert themselves.
  - **Independent**: Valuing their freedom, Aries individuals prefer to forge their own path. They are self-reliant and enjoy taking initiative.
  - **Passionate**: Driven by their desires, Aries people are passionate and enthusiastic. They put their heart into everything they do.
- **Challenges:**
  - **Impulsive**: The same energy that drives Aries can also lead to impulsiveness. They may act without thinking, leading to hasty decisions.
  - **Impatient**: Aries individuals often want results quickly and can become frustrated with delays or obstacles.

- ◦ **Competitive**: Highly competitive, Aries may sometimes prioritize winning over collaboration, which can strain relationships.
- ◦ **Short-Tempered**: With their fiery nature, Aries can be prone to anger and may struggle with patience.
- ◦ **Self-Centered**: Aries' focus on their own goals and desires can sometimes come across as selfish or inconsiderate of others.
- **Aries in Relationships**: In relationships, Aries is passionate and dynamic. They bring excitement and spontaneity to their partnerships but may need to work on patience and consideration for their partner's needs.
- **Aries in Career**: Professionally, Aries excels in roles that require leadership, innovation, and action. They thrive in fast-paced environments and are natural entrepreneurs, soldiers, athletes, and pioneers in various fields.

Hemp for Aries: Energy and Assertiveness

Hemp, particularly products containing CBD, can support Aries individuals by promoting relaxation, reducing anxiety, and balancing their fiery energy. Here are some ways hemp can help Aries harness their strengths and address their challenges:

- **Boosting Energy**: Aries' boundless energy can be both a strength and a challenge. Hemp products, such as hemp protein powder, can provide a natural energy boost without the jitters associated with caffeine. Incorporating hemp protein into smoothies or snacks can help Aries maintain their energy levels throughout the day.
- **Promoting Relaxation**: Aries' high energy and drive can lead to stress and burnout. CBD's anxiolytic properties can help reduce stress and promote relaxation, allowing Aries to recharge and

maintain balance. Using CBD oil or capsules can provide a sense of calm and prevent burnout.

- **Supporting Focus and Clarity**: Aries' impulsiveness and impatience can benefit from enhanced focus and clarity. CBD can improve mental clarity and concentration, helping Aries stay on track and make more thoughtful decisions. Incorporating CBD into their daily routine can support focus during work or personal projects.

- **Enhancing Sleep Quality**: Adequate rest is crucial for Aries to recharge their energy. CBD can help improve sleep quality by promoting relaxation and reducing insomnia. Using CBD before bedtime can help Aries achieve restful sleep and wake up refreshed and ready to tackle new challenges.

- **Managing Emotions**: Aries' short temper and impulsiveness can be balanced with emotional regulation. CBD can help regulate mood and promote emotional balance, allowing Aries to approach situations with a calm and measured response.

Rituals and Practices for Aries Individuals

To harness their pioneering spirit and maintain balance, Aries individuals can incorporate the following rituals and practices into their routine:

Morning Energy Boost

- **CBD-Infused Smoothie**: Start the day with a CBD-infused smoothie to boost energy and maintain focus. Blend hemp protein powder, fresh fruits, spinach, and a few drops of CBD oil. This nutritious and energizing smoothie can help Aries stay fueled and focused throughout the day.

Physical Activity and Exercise

- **High-Intensity Workouts**: Aries thrives on physical activity and competition. Engage in high-intensity workouts like running, martial arts, or CrossFit to channel their energy and maintain physical fitness. Use CBD topicals to soothe muscles and reduce inflammation after workouts.
- **Yoga for Balance**: Incorporate yoga into the routine to promote flexibility, balance, and relaxation. Focus on poses that build strength and calm the mind. Use CBD to enhance relaxation and focus during yoga practice.

Mindfulness and Meditation

- **Guided Meditation**: Practice guided meditation to promote relaxation and mental clarity. Use CBD to enhance relaxation and focus. Find a quiet space, sit comfortably, and listen to a guided meditation that focuses on grounding and balance.
- **Breathwork Exercises**: Engage in breathwork exercises to calm the mind and regulate emotions. Practice deep, intentional breathing to reduce stress and improve focus. Use CBD to enhance relaxation during breathwork sessions.

Creative Expression

- **Artistic Projects**: Aries' passion and creativity can be channeled into artistic projects. Engage in painting, drawing, or crafting to express emotions and ideas. Use CBD to reduce anxiety and enhance creative flow.
- **Writing and Journaling**: Keep a journal to reflect on experiences, goals, and emotions. Use a hemp journal and CBD to promote relaxation and clarity while writing. Reflect on personal growth and set intentions for future endeavors.

Goal Setting and Planning

- **Vision Boarding**: Create a vision board to visualize goals and aspirations. Use images, quotes, and symbols that resonate with Aries' ambitions. Place the vision board in a prominent location as a daily reminder of their path. Use CBD to promote relaxation and focus while creating the vision board.
- **Goal Tracking**: Set specific, measurable goals and track progress regularly. Use a planner or digital tool to stay organized and motivated. Incorporate CBD into the routine to maintain focus and reduce stress while working towards goals.

Self-Care and Relaxation

- **Relaxing Bath Ritual**: Create a relaxing bath ritual using CBD-infused bath bombs or salts. Add calming essential oils like lavender or eucalyptus. Soak in the warm water, reflecting on the day's achievements and releasing any stress or tension.
- **Mindful Eating**: Practice mindful eating to nourish the body and mind. Choose nutritious, whole foods and savor each bite. Use CBD to promote relaxation and enhance the mindful eating experience.

Social and Community Engagement

- **Group Activities**: Engage in group activities that promote camaraderie and teamwork. Join clubs, sports teams, or community organizations that align with Aries' interests. Use CBD to manage social anxiety and enhance positive interactions.
- **Volunteering**: Participate in volunteer work or community service projects. Use CBD to maintain emotional balance and promote a positive mindset while helping others. Reflect on the impact of their contributions and the sense of fulfillment gained from giving back.

Personal Development

- **Learning and Exploration**: Embrace the Aries spirit of exploration by learning new skills or pursuing new interests. Take classes, attend workshops, or engage in self-directed learning. Use CBD to enhance focus and reduce stress during the learning process.
- **Adventure and Travel**: Plan adventures or travel experiences that align with Aries' love for excitement and new experiences. Use CBD to manage travel-related stress and enhance enjoyment. Reflect on the lessons and insights gained from these experiences.

Emotional Regulation

- **Affirmation Practice**: Practice positive affirmations to reinforce confidence and emotional balance. Write down affirmations like "I am courageous and capable" or "I approach challenges with calm and confidence." Repeat these affirmations daily to cultivate a positive mindset.
- **Conflict Resolution**: Develop conflict resolution skills to manage Aries' fiery temper. Use CBD to promote calm and focus during difficult conversations. Practice active listening, empathy, and assertive communication to resolve conflicts constructively.

In this chapter, we have explored the characteristics and traits of Aries, the benefits of using hemp to support their energy and assertiveness, and various rituals and practices to enhance their pioneering spirit. By understanding the dynamic nature of Aries and incorporating hemp products into their routine, Aries individuals can harness their strengths, balance their challenges, and achieve personal and professional growth. As we continue our journey through this book, we will discover more ways to integrate hemp and astrology for holistic healing and personal development.

Check out my Virtual dispensary for all your hemp needs: https://shift.store/sg1fan23477/retail

Chapter 26: Taurus: The Sensualist
Characteristics and Traits of Taurus

Taurus, the second sign of the zodiac, is known for its grounded and sensual nature. Ruled by Venus, the planet of love and beauty, Taurus embodies stability, practicality, and a deep appreciation for life's pleasures. This fixed earth sign values comfort, security, and the finer things in life, often displaying a strong connection to nature and a keen aesthetic sense.

- **Positive Traits:**
  - **Dependable**: Taurus individuals are reliable and responsible. They are often seen as the rock in their relationships and can be counted on to follow through on commitments.
  - **Patient**: With a steady and patient nature, Taurus people are not easily rushed. They take their time to ensure that things are done correctly and thoroughly.
  - **Practical**: Taurus is grounded in reality and prefers practical solutions. They have a knack for managing resources and are often excellent at handling finances and planning.
  - **Loyal**: Once they commit, Taurus individuals are fiercely loyal. They value long-term relationships and friendships and are dedicated to those they care about.
  - **Sensual**: Ruled by Venus, Taurus has a deep appreciation for sensory experiences. They love beauty, comfort, and luxury, and they enjoy indulging in life's pleasures.
- **Challenges:**
  - **Stubborn**: Taurus's determination can sometimes turn into stubbornness. They may resist change and be reluctant to let go of familiar routines and habits.

- ○ **Possessive**: Taurus's desire for security can lead to possessiveness in relationships and material possessions. They may struggle with jealousy and a need for control.
  - ○ **Materialistic**: With a strong appreciation for luxury and comfort, Taurus can sometimes place too much importance on material wealth and physical possessions.
  - ○ **Slow to Change**: Taurus's preference for stability can make them resistant to change. They may need extra time to adapt to new situations or ideas.
  - ○ **Overindulgent**: Their love for sensory pleasures can sometimes lead to overindulgence in food, drink, or other comforts.
- **Taurus in Relationships**: In relationships, Taurus is loyal, affectionate, and devoted. They value stability and are willing to work hard to maintain a harmonious partnership. They appreciate romantic gestures and enjoy creating a comfortable, loving environment for their partner.
- **Taurus in Career**: Professionally, Taurus excels in roles that require patience, persistence, and practicality. They thrive in careers related to finance, real estate, art, and design. Their meticulous nature and eye for detail make them excellent at managing resources and projects.

Hemp for Taurus: Relaxation and Pleasure

Hemp, particularly products containing CBD, can enhance Taurus individuals' experiences by promoting relaxation, reducing stress, and enhancing their enjoyment of life's pleasures. Here are some ways hemp can support Taurus in aligning with their natural traits and addressing their challenges:

- **Promoting Relaxation**: Taurus individuals value relaxation and comfort. CBD's calming properties can help reduce stress and promote a sense of tranquility, allowing Taurus to fully unwind and enjoy their downtime. Using CBD oil or edibles can enhance their relaxation rituals and support their overall well-being.

- **Enhancing Sensory Experiences**: Taurus's appreciation for sensory pleasures can be heightened with hemp products. CBD-infused lotions, bath bombs, and oils can enhance tactile experiences, while CBD edibles can add a new dimension to their enjoyment of food and drink.

- **Supporting Emotional Balance**: Taurus's possessiveness and resistance to change can benefit from emotional regulation. CBD can help stabilize mood and promote emotional balance, allowing Taurus to navigate challenges with greater ease and adaptability.

- **Improving Sleep Quality**: Adequate rest is crucial for Taurus to maintain their energy and well-being. CBD can help improve sleep quality by promoting relaxation and reducing insomnia. Using CBD before bedtime can help Taurus achieve restful sleep and wake up feeling refreshed.

- **Alleviating Physical Discomfort**: Taurus's love for physical comfort can be supported with CBD topicals, such as balms and creams, to alleviate pain and inflammation. This allows Taurus to stay comfortable and enjoy their favorite activities without physical discomfort.

Rituals and Practices for Taurus Individuals

To harness their sensual nature and maintain balance, Taurus individuals can incorporate the following rituals and practices into their routine:

Morning Routine

- **CBD-Infused Breakfast**: Start the day with a CBD-infused breakfast to promote relaxation and set a calm tone for the day. Add CBD oil to a smoothie or enjoy a CBD-infused granola bar. This can help Taurus maintain their steady energy and focus throughout the day.

Sensory Indulgence

- **Relaxing Bath Ritual**: Create a luxurious bath ritual using CBD-infused bath bombs or salts. Add calming essential oils like lavender or rose. Light candles and play soothing music to enhance the sensory experience. Soak in the warm water, letting go of stress and tension, and indulge in the calming atmosphere.
- **Aromatherapy and Massage**: Use CBD-infused massage oils for self-massage or with a partner. Incorporate aromatherapy with essential oils like sandalwood, patchouli, or bergamot to enhance relaxation and sensory pleasure. This practice can help Taurus unwind and connect with their sensual nature.

Mindfulness and Meditation

- **Guided Meditation**: Practice guided meditation to promote relaxation and mental clarity. Use CBD to enhance relaxation and focus. Find a quiet space, sit comfortably, and listen to a guided meditation that focuses on grounding and inner peace.
- **Gratitude Journaling**: Keep a gratitude journal to reflect on the positive aspects of life. Use a hemp journal and CBD to promote relaxation and clarity while writing. Each day, write down things you are grateful for and reflect on the abundance in your life.

Creative Expression

- **Art and Craft Projects**: Engage in creative projects like painting, drawing, or crafting to express emotions and ideas. Use CBD to reduce anxiety and enhance creative flow. Allow your intuition to guide your artistic process and enjoy the tactile pleasure of creating something with your hands.
- **Gardening and Nature**: Taurus individuals often have a strong connection to nature. Spend time gardening or simply enjoying

the outdoors. Use CBD to enhance relaxation and mindfulness while connecting with the natural world.

Goal Setting and Planning

- **Vision Boarding**: Create a vision board to visualize goals and aspirations. Use images, quotes, and symbols that resonate with Taurus's desires for stability and beauty. Place the vision board in a prominent location as a daily reminder of their path. Use CBD to promote relaxation and focus while creating the vision board.
- **Financial Planning**: Taurus's practical nature makes them excellent at managing finances. Set aside time for financial planning and goal setting. Use CBD to enhance focus and reduce stress while reviewing budgets, investments, and financial goals.

Self-Care and Relaxation

- **Spa Day at Home**: Create a spa day at home using CBD-infused products. Enjoy a facial mask, body scrub, and relaxing bath. Use CBD lotions and oils for self-massage. This practice can help Taurus feel pampered and rejuvenated.
- **Mindful Eating**: Practice mindful eating to savor and appreciate food fully. Choose nutritious, whole foods and savor each bite. Use CBD to promote relaxation and enhance the mindful eating experience.

Social and Community Engagement

- **Hosting Gatherings**: Taurus individuals enjoy socializing in comfortable settings. Host gatherings with friends and family, incorporating CBD-infused foods and drinks. Create a relaxing and inviting atmosphere for your guests to enjoy.

- **Volunteering and Community Service**: Engage in volunteer work or community service projects. Use CBD to manage stress and maintain emotional balance while helping others. Reflect on the sense of fulfillment and connection gained from giving back.

Personal Development

- **Learning and Exploration**: Embrace the Taurus love for knowledge and beauty by learning new skills or exploring new interests. Take classes, attend workshops, or engage in self-directed learning. Use CBD to enhance focus and reduce stress during the learning process.
- **Travel and Adventure**: Plan adventures or travel experiences that align with Taurus's love for luxury and comfort. Use CBD to manage travel-related stress and enhance enjoyment. Reflect on the lessons and insights gained from these experiences.

Emotional Regulation

- **Affirmation Practice**: Practice positive affirmations to reinforce confidence and emotional balance. Write down affirmations like "I am grounded and secure" or "I embrace change with grace." Repeat these affirmations daily to cultivate a positive mindset.
- **Conflict Resolution**: Develop conflict resolution skills to manage Taurus's stubbornness and possessiveness. Use CBD to promote calm and focus during difficult conversations. Practice active listening, empathy, and assertive communication to resolve conflicts constructively.

In this chapter, we have explored the characteristics and traits of Taurus, the benefits of using hemp to support their relaxation and pleasure, and various rituals and practices to enhance their sensual nature. By understanding the grounded and practical nature of Taurus and incorporating hemp products into their routine, Taurus individuals can harness their strengths, balance their challenges, and achieve personal and professional growth. As we continue our journey through this book, we will discover more ways to integrate hemp and astrology for holistic healing and personal development.

Check out my Virtual dispensary for all your hemp needs: https://shift.store/sg1fan23477/retail

Chapter 27: Gemini: The Communicator
Characteristics and Traits of Gemini

Gemini, the third sign of the zodiac, is known for its versatility, curiosity, and communicative nature. Ruled by Mercury, the planet of communication and intellect, Gemini embodies adaptability, quick thinking, and a love for learning. This mutable air sign is often seen as dynamic and engaging, with a natural ability to connect with others and share ideas.

- **Positive Traits:**
  - **Curious:** Gemini individuals have a deep curiosity about the world. They love learning new things, exploring new ideas, and staying informed about current events.
  - **Adaptable:** With their mutable nature, Geminis can easily adapt to changing circumstances. They are flexible and can thrive in a variety of environments.
  - **Communicative:** Geminis are skilled communicators, both verbally and in writing. They enjoy engaging in conversations, sharing their knowledge, and connecting with others.
  - **Quick-Witted:** Known for their sharp intellect, Geminis can think on their feet and come up with clever solutions. They enjoy mental challenges and problem-solving.
  - **Sociable:** Geminis are naturally sociable and enjoy being around people. They thrive in social settings and are often the life of the party.
- **Challenges:**
  - **Indecisive:** Gemini's love for variety can lead to indecisiveness. They may struggle to commit to one course of action or decision.
  - **Superficial:** Their curiosity can sometimes lead to a lack of depth. Geminis may skim the surface of topics without fully diving into details.

- ○ **Restless**: With their active minds, Geminis can become easily bored and restless. They may have difficulty sticking to long-term projects.
- ○ **Inconsistent**: Gemini's adaptability can sometimes result in inconsistency. They may start projects with enthusiasm but lose interest quickly.
- ○ **Nervous**: Their mental activity can lead to anxiety and nervousness. Geminis may struggle with overthinking and mental exhaustion.

- **Gemini in Relationships**: In relationships, Gemini is playful, engaging, and communicative. They bring excitement and variety to their partnerships but may need to work on commitment and depth. They value intellectual connections and enjoy stimulating conversations with their partners.
- **Gemini in Career**: Professionally, Gemini excels in roles that require communication, adaptability, and mental agility. They thrive in careers related to journalism, teaching, writing, marketing, and public relations. Their ability to multitask and think quickly makes them valuable in dynamic environments.

Hemp for Gemini: Mental Clarity and Social Engagement

Hemp, particularly products containing CBD, can support Gemini individuals by promoting mental clarity, reducing anxiety, and enhancing their social experiences. Here are some ways hemp can help Gemini harness their strengths and address their challenges:

- **Promoting Mental Clarity**: Gemini's active mind can benefit from enhanced focus and clarity. CBD can help improve concentration and reduce mental fog, allowing Gemini to stay sharp and engaged. Using CBD oil or capsules can support mental clarity during work or personal projects.
- **Reducing Anxiety**: Gemini's nervous energy and tendency to overthink can lead to anxiety. CBD's anxiolytic properties can

help reduce anxiety and promote a sense of calm, allowing Gemini to approach situations with a clear and composed mind.

- **Enhancing Social Engagement**: Geminis thrive in social settings, and CBD can help reduce social anxiety and enhance their enjoyment of interactions. Using CBD before social events can promote relaxation and confidence, making it easier for Gemini to connect with others.
- **Supporting Emotional Balance**: Emotional stability is crucial for Gemini to manage their restlessness and inconsistency. CBD can help regulate mood and promote emotional balance, allowing Gemini to navigate their emotions with greater ease.
- **Improving Sleep Quality**: Adequate rest is essential for Gemini to recharge their energy and maintain mental clarity. CBD can help improve sleep quality by promoting relaxation and reducing insomnia. Using CBD before bedtime can help Gemini achieve restful sleep and wake up feeling refreshed.

Rituals and Practices for Gemini Individuals

To harness their communicative nature and maintain balance, Gemini individuals can incorporate the following rituals and practices into their routine:

Morning Routine

- **CBD-Infused Breakfast**: Start the day with a CBD-infused breakfast to promote mental clarity and set a calm tone for the day. Add CBD oil to a smoothie or enjoy a CBD-infused granola bar. This can help Gemini maintain their energy and focus throughout the day.

Mindfulness and Meditation

- **Guided Meditation**: Practice guided meditation to promote mental clarity and relaxation. Use CBD to enhance relaxation and focus. Find a quiet space, sit comfortably, and listen to a guided meditation that focuses on calming the mind and enhancing concentration.

- **Breathwork Exercises**: Engage in breathwork exercises to calm the mind and reduce anxiety. Practice deep, intentional breathing to improve focus and mental clarity. Use CBD to enhance relaxation during breathwork sessions.

Creative Expression

- **Writing and Journaling**: Keep a journal to reflect on experiences, thoughts, and ideas. Use a hemp journal and CBD to promote relaxation and clarity while writing. Reflect on personal growth, set intentions, and explore new ideas.
- **Artistic Projects**: Engage in creative projects like painting, drawing, or crafting to express emotions and ideas. Use CBD to reduce anxiety and enhance creative flow. Allow your intuition to guide your artistic process and enjoy the tactile pleasure of creating something with your hands.

Goal Setting and Planning

- **Vision Boarding**: Create a vision board to visualize goals and aspirations. Use images, quotes, and symbols that resonate with Gemini's intellectual and social interests. Place the vision board in a prominent location as a daily reminder of their path. Use CBD to promote relaxation and focus while creating the vision board.
- **Task Management**: Set specific, measurable goals and track progress regularly. Use a planner or digital tool to stay organized and motivated. Incorporate CBD into the routine to maintain focus and reduce stress while working towards goals.

Social Engagement

- **Hosting Gatherings**: Geminis enjoy socializing and connecting with others. Host gatherings with friends and family, incorporating CBD-infused foods and drinks. Create a relaxing and inviting atmosphere for your guests to enjoy stimulating conversations.
- **Joining Clubs and Groups**: Engage in social clubs or interest groups that align with Gemini's passions. Use CBD to manage social anxiety and enhance positive interactions. Participate in group activities and enjoy the sense of community and connection.

Learning and Exploration

- **Continual Learning**: Embrace Gemini's love for knowledge by continually learning new skills or exploring new interests. Take classes, attend workshops, or engage in self-directed learning. Use CBD to enhance focus and reduce stress during the learning process.
- **Travel and Adventure**: Plan adventures or travel experiences that align with Gemini's love for variety and exploration. Use CBD to manage travel-related stress and enhance enjoyment. Reflect on the lessons and insights gained from these experiences.

Self-Care and Relaxation

- **Relaxing Bath Ritual**: Create a relaxing bath ritual using CBD-infused bath bombs or salts. Add calming essential oils like lavender or chamomile. Light candles and play soothing music to enhance the sensory experience. Soak in the warm water, letting go of stress and tension.
- **Mindful Eating**: Practice mindful eating to nourish the body and mind. Choose nutritious, whole foods and savor each bite.

Use CBD to promote relaxation and enhance the mindful eating experience.

Personal Development

- **Positive Affirmations**: Practice positive affirmations to reinforce confidence and emotional balance. Write down affirmations like "I am clear-minded and focused" or "I embrace change with ease." Repeat these affirmations daily to cultivate a positive mindset.
- **Conflict Resolution**: Develop conflict resolution skills to manage Gemini's nervousness and indecisiveness. Use CBD to promote calm and focus during difficult conversations. Practice active listening, empathy, and assertive communication to resolve conflicts constructively.

Community Engagement

- **Volunteering and Service**: Engage in volunteer work or community service projects. Use CBD to manage stress and maintain emotional balance while helping others. Reflect on the sense of fulfillment and connection gained from giving back.
- **Public Speaking and Networking**: Gemini's communication skills can be honed through public speaking and networking events. Use CBD to reduce anxiety and enhance confidence. Practice speeches, engage in discussions, and build connections within your community.

In this chapter, we have explored the characteristics and traits of Gemini, the benefits of using hemp to support their mental clarity and social engagement, and various rituals and practices to enhance their communicative nature. By understanding the dynamic and intellectual nature of Gemini and incorporating hemp products into their routine, Gemini individuals can harness their strengths, balance their challenges, and achieve personal and professional growth. As we continue our journey through this book, we will discover more ways to integrate hemp and astrology for holistic healing and personal development.

Check out my Virtual dispensary for all your hemp needs: https://shift.store/sg1fan23477/retail

Chapter 28: Cancer: The Nurturer
Characteristics and Traits of Cancer

Cancer, the fourth sign of the zodiac, is known for its nurturing and compassionate nature. Ruled by the Moon, Cancer embodies sensitivity, intuition, and a deep connection to home and family. This cardinal water sign is often seen as empathetic and protective, with a natural ability to care for others and create a sense of security and comfort.

- **Positive Traits:**
  - **Compassionate**: Cancer individuals have a deep sense of empathy and compassion. They are sensitive to the emotions of others and are always willing to lend a helping hand.
  - **Intuitive**: Ruled by the Moon, Cancers have strong intuition and can often sense what others are feeling. They trust their gut instincts and have a deep connection to their inner selves.
  - **Nurturing**: Cancer is the caregiver of the zodiac. They take great pleasure in nurturing and supporting their loved ones, often putting the needs of others before their own.
  - **Protective**: Cancers are fiercely protective of their family and friends. They create a safe and secure environment for those they care about and are always ready to defend their loved ones.
  - **Loyal**: Cancer individuals are loyal and devoted. They value long-term relationships and are committed to maintaining strong bonds with their loved ones.
- **Challenges:**
  - **Moody**: Cancer's sensitivity can sometimes lead to moodiness. They may experience frequent emotional ups and downs and can be easily hurt by the actions of others.

- **Overly Protective**: While their protective nature is a strength, it can sometimes become overbearing. Cancers may struggle with letting go and allowing their loved ones to grow independently.
  - **Insecure**: Cancer individuals may struggle with self-doubt and insecurity. They may seek constant reassurance and validation from others.
  - **Clingy**: Cancer's deep need for connection can sometimes lead to clinginess. They may have difficulty giving their loved ones space and independence.
  - **Retreating**: When hurt or overwhelmed, Cancers may retreat into their shells, isolating themselves from others. They may struggle with expressing their emotions openly.
- **Cancer in Relationships**: In relationships, Cancer is caring, affectionate, and devoted. They value emotional connection and are deeply committed to their partners. They create a nurturing and supportive environment but may need to work on managing their moodiness and need for reassurance.
- **Cancer in Career**: Professionally, Cancer excels in roles that require empathy, caregiving, and intuition. They thrive in careers related to healthcare, counseling, social work, and hospitality. Their ability to connect with others and provide support makes them valuable in any role that involves nurturing and caring for others.

Hemp for Cancer: Emotional Balance and Comfort

Hemp, particularly products containing CBD, can support Cancer individuals by promoting emotional balance, reducing anxiety, and enhancing their sense of comfort and security. Here are some ways hemp can help Cancer harness their strengths and address their challenges:

- **Promoting Emotional Balance**: Cancer's sensitivity and moodiness can benefit from enhanced emotional regulation. CBD can help stabilize mood and promote emotional balance, allowing Cancer to navigate their feelings with greater ease.

- **Reducing Anxiety**: Cancer's tendency to worry and seek reassurance can lead to anxiety. CBD's anxiolytic properties can help reduce anxiety and promote a sense of calm, allowing Cancer to approach situations with a clear and composed mind.
- **Enhancing Comfort and Relaxation**: Cancer individuals value comfort and security. CBD can help promote relaxation and enhance their sense of well-being, making it easier for Cancer to create a nurturing environment for themselves and their loved ones.
- **Improving Sleep Quality**: Adequate rest is crucial for Cancer to maintain their emotional well-being. CBD can help improve sleep quality by promoting relaxation and reducing insomnia. Using CBD before bedtime can help Cancer achieve restful sleep and wake up feeling refreshed.
- **Alleviating Physical Discomfort**: Cancer's desire for physical comfort can be supported with CBD topicals, such as balms and creams, to alleviate pain and inflammation. This allows Cancer to stay comfortable and enjoy their favorite activities without physical discomfort.

Rituals and Practices for Cancer Individuals

To harness their nurturing nature and maintain balance, Cancer individuals can incorporate the following rituals and practices into their routine:

Morning Routine

- **CBD-Infused Breakfast**: Start the day with a CBD-infused breakfast to promote emotional balance and set a calm tone for the day. Add CBD oil to a smoothie or enjoy a CBD-infused granola bar. This can help Cancer maintain their energy and focus throughout the day.

Nurturing and Self-Care

- **Relaxing Bath Ritual**: Create a luxurious bath ritual using CBD-infused bath bombs or salts. Add calming essential oils like lavender or chamomile. Light candles and play soothing music to enhance the sensory experience. Soak in the warm water, letting go of stress and tension, and indulge in the calming atmosphere.
- **Aromatherapy and Massage**: Use CBD-infused massage oils for self-massage or with a partner. Incorporate aromatherapy with essential oils like rose, jasmine, or sandalwood to enhance relaxation and sensory pleasure. This practice can help Cancer unwind and connect with their nurturing nature.

Mindfulness and Meditation

- **Guided Meditation**: Practice guided meditation to promote emotional balance and relaxation. Use CBD to enhance relaxation and focus. Find a quiet space, sit comfortably, and listen to a guided meditation that focuses on calming the mind and enhancing emotional stability.
- **Breathwork Exercises**: Engage in breathwork exercises to calm the mind and reduce anxiety. Practice deep, intentional breathing to improve focus and emotional regulation. Use CBD to enhance relaxation during breathwork sessions.

Creative Expression

- **Art and Craft Projects**: Engage in creative projects like painting, drawing, or crafting to express emotions and ideas. Use CBD to reduce anxiety and enhance creative flow. Allow your intuition to guide your artistic process and enjoy the tactile pleasure of creating something with your hands.

- **Cooking and Baking**: Cancer individuals often enjoy cooking and baking as a form of nurturing. Use CBD-infused recipes to create delicious and comforting meals for yourself and your loved ones. Enjoy the process of preparing and sharing food as a way to connect and nurture.

Goal Setting and Planning

- **Vision Boarding**: Create a vision board to visualize goals and aspirations. Use images, quotes, and symbols that resonate with Cancer's desire for emotional connection and security. Place the vision board in a prominent location as a daily reminder of their path. Use CBD to promote relaxation and focus while creating the vision board.
- **Task Management**: Set specific, measurable goals and track progress regularly. Use a planner or digital tool to stay organized and motivated. Incorporate CBD into the routine to maintain focus and reduce stress while working towards goals.

Social Engagement

- **Hosting Gatherings**: Cancer individuals enjoy creating a nurturing and welcoming environment for their loved ones. Host gatherings with friends and family, incorporating CBD-infused foods and drinks. Create a relaxing and inviting atmosphere for your guests to enjoy.
- **Joining Support Groups**: Engage in support groups or interest groups that align with Cancer's nurturing nature. Use CBD to manage social anxiety and enhance positive interactions. Participate in group activities and enjoy the sense of community and connection.

Learning and Exploration

- **Continual Learning**: Embrace Cancer's love for knowledge and personal growth by continually learning new skills or exploring new interests. Take classes, attend workshops, or engage in self-directed learning. Use CBD to enhance focus and reduce stress during the learning process.
- **Travel and Adventure**: Plan adventures or travel experiences that align with Cancer's love for comfort and connection. Use CBD to manage travel-related stress and enhance enjoyment. Reflect on the lessons and insights gained from these experiences.

Self-Care and Relaxation

- **Spa Day at Home**: Create a spa day at home using CBD-infused products. Enjoy a facial mask, body scrub, and relaxing bath. Use CBD lotions and oils for self-massage. This practice can help Cancer feel pampered and rejuvenated.
- **Mindful Eating**: Practice mindful eating to nourish the body and mind. Choose nutritious, whole foods and savor each bite. Use CBD to promote relaxation and enhance the mindful eating experience.

Personal Development

- **Positive Affirmations**: Practice positive affirmations to reinforce confidence and emotional balance. Write down affirmations like "I am strong and compassionate" or "I nurture myself and others with love." Repeat these affirmations daily to cultivate a positive mindset.
- **Conflict Resolution**: Develop conflict resolution skills to manage Cancer's moodiness and need for reassurance. Use CBD to promote calm and focus during difficult conversations. Practice active listening, empathy, and assertive communication to resolve conflicts constructively.

Community Engagement

- **Volunteering and Service**: Engage in volunteer work or community service projects. Use CBD to manage stress and maintain emotional balance while helping others. Reflect on the sense of fulfillment and connection gained from giving back.
- **Public Speaking and Networking**: Cancer's nurturing skills can be honed through public speaking and networking events. Use CBD to reduce anxiety and enhance confidence. Practice speeches, engage in discussions, and build connections within your community.

In this chapter, we have explored the characteristics and traits of Cancer, the benefits of using hemp to support their emotional balance and comfort, and various rituals and practices to enhance their nurturing nature. By understanding the compassionate and intuitive nature of Cancer and incorporating hemp products into their routine, Cancer individuals can harness their strengths, balance their challenges, and achieve personal and professional growth. As we continue our journey through this book, we will discover more ways to integrate hemp and astrology for holistic healing and personal development.

Check out my Virtual dispensary for all your hemp needs: https://shift.store/sg1fan23477/retail

Chapter 29: Leo: The Leader
Characteristics and Traits of Leo

Leo, the fifth sign of the zodiac, is known for its vibrant and charismatic nature. Ruled by the Sun, Leo embodies confidence, creativity, and a natural flair for leadership. This fixed fire sign is often seen as generous, warm-hearted, and enthusiastic, with a strong desire to shine and be recognized for their talents.

- **Positive Traits**:
  - **Confident**: Leo individuals have a natural confidence that draws others to them. They believe in their abilities and are not afraid to take the spotlight.
  - **Creative**: Leos are highly creative and have a strong artistic flair. They enjoy expressing themselves through various forms of art, performance, and innovation.
  - **Generous**: With big hearts, Leos are generous and giving. They love to share their time, resources, and affection with others.
  - **Passionate**: Leos are passionate about their interests and pursuits. They throw themselves wholeheartedly into everything they do and inspire others with their enthusiasm.
  - **Leadership**: Natural leaders, Leos are comfortable in positions of authority and enjoy guiding and motivating others. They have a strong sense of purpose and direction.
- **Challenges**:
  - **Arrogant**: Leo's confidence can sometimes turn into arrogance. They may come across as overly proud or self-centered.

- ○ **Stubborn**: As a fixed sign, Leos can be stubborn and resistant to change. They may struggle to adapt to new situations or perspectives.
- ○ **Attention-Seeking**: Leos crave recognition and may become upset if they feel overlooked or unappreciated. They need to feel valued and admired.
- ○ **Dramatic**: With a flair for the dramatic, Leos can sometimes blow things out of proportion. They may struggle with managing their reactions and emotions.
- ○ **Dominant**: Leo's natural leadership can sometimes turn into dominance. They may have difficulty delegating or allowing others to take the lead.
- **Leo in Relationships**: In relationships, Leo is warm, affectionate, and loyal. They bring excitement and passion to their partnerships and enjoy showering their loved ones with attention and gifts. They need to work on balancing their need for admiration with giving their partners space and recognition.
- **Leo in Career**: Professionally, Leo excels in roles that require leadership, creativity, and public presence. They thrive in careers related to entertainment, arts, management, and public relations. Their charisma and confidence make them natural leaders and motivators.

Hemp for Leo: Confidence and Creativity

Hemp, particularly products containing CBD, can support Leo individuals by enhancing their confidence, boosting creativity, and helping them manage stress. Here are some ways hemp can help Leo harness their strengths and address their challenges:

- **Boosting Confidence**: Leo's natural confidence can be further enhanced with the calming and balancing effects of CBD. Using CBD can help reduce anxiety and promote a sense of calm, allowing Leo to step into their leadership roles with even greater assurance.

- **Enhancing Creativity**: Leos thrive on creative expression. CBD can help reduce mental fog and enhance focus, allowing Leo to channel their creative energy more effectively. Incorporating CBD into their daily routine can support their artistic and innovative pursuits.
- **Managing Stress**: Leo's leadership roles and desire for recognition can sometimes lead to stress. CBD's anxiolytic properties can help manage stress and promote relaxation, allowing Leo to approach challenges with a calm and composed mindset.
- **Supporting Emotional Balance**: Emotional stability is crucial for Leo to maintain their passion and enthusiasm without becoming overly dramatic or reactive. CBD can help regulate mood and promote emotional balance, allowing Leo to navigate their emotions with greater ease.
- **Improving Sleep Quality**: Adequate rest is essential for Leo to recharge their energy and maintain their vibrant presence. CBD can help improve sleep quality by promoting relaxation and reducing insomnia. Using CBD before bedtime can help Leo achieve restful sleep and wake up feeling refreshed.

Rituals and Practices for Leo Individuals

To harness their leadership qualities and maintain balance, Leo individuals can incorporate the following rituals and practices into their routine:

Morning Routine

- **CBD-Infused Breakfast**: Start the day with a CBD-infused breakfast to promote confidence and set a positive tone for the day. Add CBD oil to a smoothie or enjoy a CBD-infused granola bar. This can help Leo maintain their energy and focus throughout the day.

Creative Expression

- **Artistic Projects**: Engage in creative projects like painting, drawing, writing, or performing arts to express emotions and ideas. Use CBD to reduce anxiety and enhance creative flow. Allow your intuition to guide your artistic process and enjoy the satisfaction of creating something unique.
- **Vision Boarding**: Create a vision board to visualize goals and aspirations. Use images, quotes, and symbols that resonate with Leo's ambitions and desires. Place the vision board in a prominent location as a daily reminder of their path. Use CBD to promote relaxation and focus while creating the vision board.

Leadership and Goal Setting

- **Leadership Development**: Embrace Leo's natural leadership skills by engaging in leadership development activities. Take classes, attend workshops, or read books on leadership and personal growth. Use CBD to enhance focus and reduce stress during these learning experiences.
- **Task Management**: Set specific, measurable goals and track progress regularly. Use a planner or digital tool to stay organized and motivated. Incorporate CBD into the routine to maintain focus and reduce stress while working towards goals.

Mindfulness and Meditation

- **Guided Meditation**: Practice guided meditation to promote emotional balance and relaxation. Use CBD to enhance relaxation and focus. Find a quiet space, sit comfortably, and listen to a guided meditation that focuses on boosting confidence and calming the mind.

- **Breathwork Exercises**: Engage in breathwork exercises to calm the mind and reduce anxiety. Practice deep, intentional breathing to improve focus and emotional regulation. Use CBD to enhance relaxation during breathwork sessions.

Social Engagement

- **Hosting Gatherings**: Leos enjoy socializing and being in the spotlight. Host gatherings with friends and family, incorporating CBD-infused foods and drinks. Create a fun and inviting atmosphere for your guests to enjoy stimulating conversations and entertainment.
- **Joining Clubs and Groups**: Engage in social clubs or interest groups that align with Leo's passions. Use CBD to manage social anxiety and enhance positive interactions. Participate in group activities and enjoy the sense of community and connection.

Personal Development

- **Positive Affirmations**: Practice positive affirmations to reinforce confidence and emotional balance. Write down affirmations like "I am a confident and inspiring leader" or "I express my creativity with passion." Repeat these affirmations daily to cultivate a positive mindset.
- **Conflict Resolution**: Develop conflict resolution skills to manage Leo's dominance and need for recognition. Use CBD to promote calm and focus during difficult conversations. Practice active listening, empathy, and assertive communication to resolve conflicts constructively.

Self-Care and Relaxation

- **Spa Day at Home**: Create a spa day at home using CBD-infused products. Enjoy a facial mask, body scrub, and relaxing bath. Use CBD lotions and oils for self-massage. This practice can help Leo feel pampered and rejuvenated.
- **Mindful Eating**: Practice mindful eating to nourish the body and mind. Choose nutritious, whole foods and savor each bite. Use CBD to promote relaxation and enhance the mindful eating experience.

Learning and Exploration

- **Continual Learning**: Embrace Leo's love for knowledge and personal growth by continually learning new skills or exploring new interests. Take classes, attend workshops, or engage in self-directed learning. Use CBD to enhance focus and reduce stress during the learning process.
- **Travel and Adventure**: Plan adventures or travel experiences that align with Leo's love for excitement and new experiences. Use CBD to manage travel-related stress and enhance enjoyment. Reflect on the lessons and insights gained from these experiences.

Community Engagement

- **Volunteering and Service**: Engage in volunteer work or community service projects. Use CBD to manage stress and maintain emotional balance while helping others. Reflect on the sense of fulfillment and connection gained from giving back.
- **Public Speaking and Networking**: Leo's leadership and communication skills can be honed through public speaking and networking events. Use CBD to reduce anxiety and enhance confidence. Practice speeches, engage in discussions, and build connections within your community.

Emotional and Physical Health

- **Yoga and Physical Exercise**: Incorporate physical exercise, such as yoga, into the routine to promote physical health and emotional well-being. Use CBD to alleviate muscle soreness and enhance relaxation after workouts.
- **Journaling**: Keep a journal to reflect on experiences, thoughts, and ideas. Use a hemp journal and CBD to promote relaxation and clarity while writing. Reflect on personal growth, set intentions, and explore new ideas.

In this chapter, we have explored the characteristics and traits of Leo, the benefits of using hemp to support their confidence and creativity, and various rituals and practices to enhance their leadership qualities. By understanding the vibrant and charismatic nature of Leo and incorporating hemp products into their routine, Leo individuals can harness their strengths, balance their challenges, and achieve personal and professional growth. As we continue our journey through this book, we will discover more ways to integrate hemp and astrology for holistic healing and personal development.

Check out my Virtual dispensary for all your hemp needs: https://shift.store/sg1fan23477/retail

Chapter 30: Virgo: The Analyst
Characteristics and Traits of Virgo

Virgo, the sixth sign of the zodiac, is known for its analytical and meticulous nature. Ruled by Mercury, the planet of communication and intellect, Virgo embodies practicality, attention to detail, and a strong desire for order and efficiency. This mutable earth sign is often seen as diligent, reliable, and intelligent, with a natural ability to organize and improve systems.

- **Positive Traits:**
  - **Detail-Oriented**: Virgos have a keen eye for detail and excel in tasks that require precision and accuracy. They are meticulous and thorough in their work.
  - **Practical**: Virgo individuals are grounded in reality and prefer practical solutions. They are skilled at problem-solving and making logical decisions.
  - **Analytical**: With their sharp intellect, Virgos are excellent analysts. They enjoy examining data, identifying patterns, and drawing insightful conclusions.
  - **Reliable**: Virgos are dependable and responsible. They take their commitments seriously and are known for their strong work ethic.
  - **Helpful**: Virgos have a strong desire to be of service to others. They are often willing to lend a helping hand and provide support when needed.
- **Challenges:**
  - **Perfectionistic**: Virgo's attention to detail can sometimes lead to perfectionism. They may set impossibly high standards for themselves and others, leading to stress and dissatisfaction.

- **Overly Critical**: Virgos' analytical nature can make them overly critical. They may focus on flaws and imperfections, which can strain relationships and affect their self-esteem.
- **Anxious**: Virgo's tendency to overthink and worry can lead to anxiety. They may struggle with managing stress and finding relaxation.
- **Reserved**: Virgos can be reserved and cautious in expressing their emotions. They may prefer to keep their feelings to themselves and have difficulty opening up to others.
- **Workaholic**: Virgo's strong work ethic can sometimes lead to workaholism. They may prioritize work over rest and relaxation, leading to burnout.

- **Virgo in Relationships**: In relationships, Virgo is caring, supportive, and attentive. They bring stability and reliability to their partnerships but may need to work on being less critical and more open in expressing their emotions. They value intellectual connections and appreciate partners who share their practical approach to life.
- **Virgo in Career**: Professionally, Virgo excels in roles that require precision, organization, and analytical thinking. They thrive in careers related to healthcare, research, administration, and quality control. Their ability to manage details and improve systems makes them valuable in any role that requires efficiency and accuracy.

Hemp for Virgo: Focus and Health

Hemp, particularly products containing CBD, can support Virgo individuals by promoting focus, reducing anxiety, and enhancing overall health. Here are some ways hemp can help Virgo harness their strengths and address their challenges:

- **Enhancing Focus**: Virgo's analytical mind can benefit from enhanced focus and clarity. CBD can help improve concentration and reduce mental fog, allowing Virgo to stay sharp and engaged. Using CBD oil or capsules can support mental clarity during work or personal projects.

- **Reducing Anxiety**: Virgo's tendency to overthink and worry can lead to anxiety. CBD's anxiolytic properties can help reduce anxiety and promote a sense of calm, allowing Virgo to approach situations with a clear and composed mind.

- **Supporting Emotional Balance**: Emotional stability is crucial for Virgo to manage their perfectionism and critical nature. CBD can help regulate mood and promote emotional balance, allowing Virgo to navigate their emotions with greater ease.

- **Improving Sleep Quality**: Adequate rest is essential for Virgo to recharge their energy and maintain their analytical sharpness. CBD can help improve sleep quality by promoting relaxation and reducing insomnia. Using CBD before bedtime can help Virgo achieve restful sleep and wake up feeling refreshed.

- **Enhancing Physical Health**: Virgo's focus on health and wellness can be supported with CBD products that promote physical well-being. CBD topicals, such as balms and creams, can help alleviate pain and inflammation, allowing Virgo to stay comfortable and active.

Rituals and Practices for Virgo Individuals

To harness their analytical nature and maintain balance, Virgo individuals can incorporate the following rituals and practices into their routine:

Morning Routine

- **CBD-Infused Breakfast**: Start the day with a CBD-infused breakfast to promote focus and set a positive tone for the day. Add CBD oil to a smoothie or enjoy a CBD-infused granola bar. This can help Virgo maintain their energy and mental clarity throughout the day.

Mindfulness and Meditation

- **Guided Meditation**: Practice guided meditation to promote relaxation and mental clarity. Use CBD to enhance relaxation and focus. Find a quiet space, sit comfortably, and listen to a guided meditation that focuses on calming the mind and enhancing concentration.
- **Breathwork Exercises**: Engage in breathwork exercises to calm the mind and reduce anxiety. Practice deep, intentional breathing to improve focus and emotional regulation. Use CBD to enhance relaxation during breathwork sessions.

Creative Expression

- **Journaling**: Keep a journal to reflect on experiences, thoughts, and ideas. Use a hemp journal and CBD to promote relaxation and clarity while writing. Reflect on personal growth, set intentions, and explore new ideas.
- **Art and Craft Projects**: Engage in creative projects like painting, drawing, or crafting to express emotions and ideas. Use CBD to reduce anxiety and enhance creative flow. Allow your intuition to guide your artistic process and enjoy the satisfaction of creating something unique.

Health and Wellness

- **Healthy Eating**: Practice mindful eating to nourish the body and mind. Choose nutritious, whole foods and savor each bite. Use CBD to promote relaxation and enhance the mindful eating experience.
- **Exercise Routine**: Incorporate regular physical exercise into the routine to promote physical health and emotional well-being.

Use CBD to alleviate muscle soreness and enhance relaxation after workouts.

Goal Setting and Planning

- **Task Management**: Set specific, measurable goals and track progress regularly. Use a planner or digital tool to stay organized and motivated. Incorporate CBD into the routine to maintain focus and reduce stress while working towards goals.
- **Vision Boarding**: Create a vision board to visualize goals and aspirations. Use images, quotes, and symbols that resonate with Virgo's practical and analytical nature. Place the vision board in a prominent location as a daily reminder of their path. Use CBD to promote relaxation and focus while creating the vision board.

Social Engagement

- **Hosting Gatherings**: Virgo individuals enjoy creating an organized and welcoming environment for their loved ones. Host gatherings with friends and family, incorporating CBD-infused foods and drinks. Create a relaxing and inviting atmosphere for your guests to enjoy.
- **Joining Clubs and Groups**: Engage in social clubs or interest groups that align with Virgo's passions. Use CBD to manage social anxiety and enhance positive interactions. Participate in group activities and enjoy the sense of community and connection.

Personal Development

- **Positive Affirmations**: Practice positive affirmations to reinforce confidence and emotional balance. Write down affirmations like "I am capable and confident" or "I embrace imperfection with grace." Repeat these affirmations daily to cultivate a positive mindset.

- **Conflict Resolution**: Develop conflict resolution skills to manage Virgo's critical nature and perfectionism. Use CBD to promote calm and focus during difficult conversations. Practice active listening, empathy, and assertive communication to resolve conflicts constructively.

Self-Care and Relaxation

- **Spa Day at Home**: Create a spa day at home using CBD-infused products. Enjoy a facial mask, body scrub, and relaxing bath. Use CBD lotions and oils for self-massage. This practice can help Virgo feel pampered and rejuvenated.
- **Relaxing Bath Ritual**: Create a relaxing bath ritual using CBD-infused bath bombs or salts. Add calming essential oils like lavender or chamomile. Light candles and play soothing music to enhance the sensory experience. Soak in the warm water, letting go of stress and tension.

Learning and Exploration

- **Continual Learning**: Embrace Virgo's love for knowledge and personal growth by continually learning new skills or exploring new interests. Take classes, attend workshops, or engage in self-directed learning. Use CBD to enhance focus and reduce stress during the learning process.
- **Travel and Adventure**: Plan adventures or travel experiences that align with Virgo's love for organization and new experiences. Use CBD to manage travel-related stress and enhance enjoyment. Reflect on the lessons and insights gained from these experiences.

Community Engagement

- **Volunteering and Service**: Engage in volunteer work or community service projects. Use CBD to manage stress and maintain emotional balance while helping others. Reflect on the sense of fulfillment and connection gained from giving back.
- **Public Speaking and Networking**: Virgo's analytical skills can be honed through public speaking and networking events. Use CBD to reduce anxiety and enhance confidence. Practice speeches, engage in discussions, and build connections within your community.

Emotional and Physical Health

- **Yoga and Physical Exercise**: Incorporate physical exercise, such as yoga, into the routine to promote physical health and emotional well-being. Use CBD to alleviate muscle soreness and enhance relaxation after workouts.
- **Health Checkups**: Regular health checkups and wellness routines can help Virgo stay on top of their physical health. Use CBD to reduce anxiety related to medical appointments and promote overall well-being.

In this chapter, we have explored the characteristics and traits of Virgo, the benefits of using hemp to support their focus and health, and various rituals and practices to enhance their analytical nature. By understanding the meticulous and practical nature of Virgo and incorporating hemp products into their routine, Virgo individuals can harness their strengths, balance their challenges, and achieve personal and professional growth. As we continue our journey through this book, we will discover more ways to integrate hemp and astrology for holistic healing and personal development.

Check out my Virtual dispensary for all your hemp needs: https://shift.store/sg1fan23477/retail

Chapter 31: Libra: The Harmonizer
Characteristics and Traits of Libra

Libra, the seventh sign of the zodiac, is known for its focus on balance, harmony, and beauty. Ruled by Venus, the planet of love and beauty, Libra embodies diplomacy, charm, and a strong desire for fairness and justice. This cardinal air sign is often seen as social, gracious, and aesthetically inclined, with a natural ability to create and maintain harmonious relationships and environments.

- **Positive Traits:**
    - **Diplomatic**: Libra individuals excel in mediation and conflict resolution. They have a talent for seeing all sides of an issue and finding fair solutions.
    - **Charming**: With their natural charm and sociability, Libras are adept at building and maintaining relationships. They are often the peacemakers in social settings.
    - **Fair-minded**: Libra values fairness and justice. They strive for equality and are committed to doing what is right.
    - **Aesthetic**: Ruled by Venus, Libras have a keen eye for beauty. They appreciate art, fashion, and design, and often have a strong sense of style.
    - **Cooperative**: Libra individuals are team players. They enjoy working with others and are skilled at fostering collaboration and cooperation.
- **Challenges:**
    - **Indecisive**: Libra's desire to weigh all options can lead to indecisiveness. They may struggle to make decisions, fearing they might upset the balance.
    - **People-Pleasing**: Libra's need for harmony can lead to people-pleasing behaviors. They may prioritize others' needs over their own to avoid conflict.

- **Avoidant**: In their quest for peace, Libras may avoid difficult conversations or decisions. This can lead to unresolved issues and suppressed emotions.
- **Superficial**: Libra's focus on beauty and aesthetics can sometimes lead to superficiality. They may prioritize appearances over deeper substance.
- **Overly Dependent**: Libras value relationships and may struggle with independence. They may rely too heavily on others for validation and support.

- **Libra in Relationships**: In relationships, Libra is affectionate, romantic, and committed to creating harmony. They bring charm and grace to their partnerships but may need to work on asserting their own needs and making decisions. They value intellectual and emotional connections and seek balanced, equitable relationships.

- **Libra in Career**: Professionally, Libra excels in roles that require diplomacy, collaboration, and a sense of aesthetics. They thrive in careers related to law, art, design, public relations, and human resources. Their ability to see all sides and foster harmony makes them valuable in any role that involves mediation and teamwork.

Hemp for Libra: Balance and Beauty

Hemp, particularly products containing CBD, can support Libra individuals by promoting balance, reducing anxiety, and enhancing their appreciation for beauty. Here are some ways hemp can help Libra harness their strengths and address their challenges:

- **Promoting Balance**: Libra's quest for balance can benefit from CBD's calming and stabilizing effects. Using CBD can help reduce stress and promote a sense of equilibrium, allowing Libra to navigate their day with greater ease.

- **Reducing Anxiety**: Libra's tendency to avoid conflict and please others can lead to anxiety. CBD's anxiolytic properties can help reduce anxiety and promote a sense of calm, allowing Libra to approach situations with confidence.

- **Enhancing Beauty Rituals**: Libra's appreciation for beauty can be enhanced with CBD-infused skincare and beauty products. CBD can help reduce inflammation, promote healthy skin, and enhance relaxation, making beauty rituals even more enjoyable.
- **Supporting Emotional Balance**: Emotional stability is crucial for Libra to maintain their harmony and avoid people-pleasing behaviors. CBD can help regulate mood and promote emotional balance, allowing Libra to assert their needs and make decisions with confidence.
- **Improving Sleep Quality**: Adequate rest is essential for Libra to recharge their energy and maintain their sense of balance. CBD can help improve sleep quality by promoting relaxation and reducing insomnia. Using CBD before bedtime can help Libra achieve restful sleep and wake up feeling refreshed.

Rituals and Practices for Libra Individuals

To harness their harmonizing qualities and maintain balance, Libra individuals can incorporate the following rituals and practices into their routine:

Morning Routine

- **CBD-Infused Breakfast**: Start the day with a CBD-infused breakfast to promote balance and set a positive tone for the day. Add CBD oil to a smoothie or enjoy a CBD-infused granola bar. This can help Libra maintain their energy and mental clarity throughout the day.

Mindfulness and Meditation

- **Guided Meditation**: Practice guided meditation to promote relaxation and mental clarity. Use CBD to enhance relaxation and focus. Find a quiet space, sit comfortably, and listen to a guided meditation that focuses on achieving balance and inner peace.

- **Breathwork Exercises**: Engage in breathwork exercises to calm the mind and reduce anxiety. Practice deep, intentional breathing to improve focus and emotional regulation. Use CBD to enhance relaxation during breathwork sessions.

Creative Expression

- **Art and Design Projects**: Engage in creative projects like painting, drawing, or interior design to express aesthetic sensibilities and emotions. Use CBD to reduce anxiety and enhance creative flow. Allow your intuition to guide your artistic process and enjoy the satisfaction of creating something beautiful.
- **Fashion and Style**: Libra's appreciation for beauty can be expressed through fashion and personal style. Experiment with different looks and use CBD to enhance relaxation and confidence while getting ready.

Health and Wellness

- **Healthy Eating**: Practice mindful eating to nourish the body and mind. Choose nutritious, whole foods and savor each bite. Use CBD to promote relaxation and enhance the mindful eating experience.
- **Exercise Routine**: Incorporate regular physical exercise into the routine to promote physical health and emotional well-being. Use CBD to alleviate muscle soreness and enhance relaxation after workouts.

Goal Setting and Planning

- **Task Management**: Set specific, measurable goals and track progress regularly. Use a planner or digital tool to stay organized and motivated. Incorporate CBD into the routine to maintain focus and reduce stress while working towards goals.
- **Vision Boarding**: Create a vision board to visualize goals and aspirations. Use images, quotes, and symbols that resonate with Libra's desire for harmony and beauty. Place the vision board in a prominent location as a daily reminder of their path. Use CBD to promote relaxation and focus while creating the vision board.

Social Engagement

- **Hosting Gatherings**: Libras enjoy socializing and creating harmonious environments for their loved ones. Host gatherings with friends and family, incorporating CBD-infused foods and drinks. Create a relaxing and inviting atmosphere for your guests to enjoy.
- **Joining Clubs and Groups**: Engage in social clubs or interest groups that align with Libra's passions. Use CBD to manage social anxiety and enhance positive interactions. Participate in group activities and enjoy the sense of community and connection.

Personal Development

- **Positive Affirmations**: Practice positive affirmations to reinforce confidence and emotional balance. Write down affirmations like "I am balanced and harmonious" or "I create beauty and peace in my life." Repeat these affirmations daily to cultivate a positive mindset.
- **Conflict Resolution**: Develop conflict resolution skills to manage Libra's avoidance tendencies and need for harmony. Use CBD to promote calm and focus during difficult conversations. Practice

active listening, empathy, and assertive communication to resolve conflicts constructively.

Self-Care and Relaxation

- **Spa Day at Home**: Create a spa day at home using CBD-infused products. Enjoy a facial mask, body scrub, and relaxing bath. Use CBD lotions and oils for self-massage. This practice can help Libra feel pampered and rejuvenated.
- **Relaxing Bath Ritual**: Create a relaxing bath ritual using CBD-infused bath bombs or salts. Add calming essential oils like lavender or rose. Light candles and play soothing music to enhance the sensory experience. Soak in the warm water, letting go of stress and tension.

Learning and Exploration

- **Continual Learning**: Embrace Libra's love for knowledge and personal growth by continually learning new skills or exploring new interests. Take classes, attend workshops, or engage in self-directed learning. Use CBD to enhance focus and reduce stress during the learning process.
- **Travel and Adventure**: Plan adventures or travel experiences that align with Libra's love for beauty and new experiences. Use CBD to manage travel-related stress and enhance enjoyment. Reflect on the lessons and insights gained from these experiences.

Community Engagement

- **Volunteering and Service**: Engage in volunteer work or community service projects. Use CBD to manage stress and maintain emotional balance while helping others. Reflect on the sense of fulfillment and connection gained from giving back.

- **Public Speaking and Networking**: Libra's diplomatic skills can be honed through public speaking and networking events. Use CBD to reduce anxiety and enhance confidence. Practice speeches, engage in discussions, and build connections within your community.

Emotional and Physical Health

- **Yoga and Physical Exercise**: Incorporate physical exercise, such as yoga, into the routine to promote physical health and emotional well-being. Use CBD to alleviate muscle soreness and enhance relaxation after workouts.
- **Health Checkups**: Regular health checkups and wellness routines can help Libra stay on top of their physical health. Use CBD to reduce anxiety related to medical appointments and promote overall well-being.

In this chapter, we have explored the characteristics and traits of Libra, the benefits of using hemp to support their balance and beauty, and various rituals and practices to enhance their harmonizing nature. By understanding the diplomatic and aesthetic nature of Libra and incorporating hemp products into their routine, Libra individuals can harness their strengths, balance their challenges, and achieve personal and professional growth. As we continue our journey through this book, we will discover more ways to integrate hemp and astrology for holistic healing and personal development.

Check out my Virtual dispensary for all your hemp needs: https://shift.store/sg1fan23477/retail

Chapter 32: Scorpio: The Transformer
Characteristics and Traits of Scorpio

Scorpio, the eighth sign of the zodiac, is known for its intensity, depth, and transformative nature. Ruled by Pluto, the planet of transformation and regeneration, and Mars, the planet of action and desire, Scorpio embodies power, passion, and mystery. This fixed water sign is often seen as resilient, resourceful, and profoundly intuitive, with a natural ability to navigate and catalyze change.

- **Positive Traits:**
  - **Intense:** Scorpio individuals have a depth of emotion and intensity that is unmatched. They approach life with passion and are not afraid to explore the darker aspects of existence.
  - **Resilient:** Scorpios possess an incredible ability to recover from setbacks. They face challenges head-on and emerge stronger, embodying the essence of transformation.
  - **Resourceful:** Scorpio's resourcefulness allows them to find solutions where others see obstacles. They are strategic thinkers who make the most of their resources.
  - **Intuitive:** With a keen sense of intuition, Scorpios can often sense hidden motives and truths. They trust their instincts and are highly perceptive.
  - **Loyal:** Scorpio individuals are fiercely loyal to those they care about. They value deep, meaningful connections and are dedicated to their loved ones.
- **Challenges:**

- ○ **Secretive**: Scorpio's private nature can sometimes lead to secrecy. They may struggle to open up and share their true feelings with others.
- ○ **Jealous**: The intensity of Scorpio's emotions can sometimes result in jealousy and possessiveness. They may need to work on trusting others and managing their fears of betrayal.
- ○ **Obsessive**: Scorpio's passion can turn into obsession. They may fixate on certain ideas, people, or goals to the detriment of their well-being.
- ○ **Stubborn**: As a fixed sign, Scorpios can be stubborn and resistant to change. They may struggle to adapt to new situations or perspectives.
- ○ **Manipulative**: Scorpio's strategic nature can sometimes turn into manipulation. They may use their understanding of others' weaknesses to achieve their own ends.

- **Scorpio in Relationships**: In relationships, Scorpio is passionate, loyal, and deeply committed. They seek profound emotional connections and value honesty and intensity in their partnerships. They bring depth and transformation to their relationships but may need to work on being more open and less controlling.
- **Scorpio in Career**: Professionally, Scorpio excels in roles that require investigation, strategy, and resilience. They thrive in careers related to psychology, research, finance, and detective work. Their ability to delve deeply and uncover hidden truths makes them valuable in any role that involves transformation and analysis.

Hemp for Scorpio: Deep Healing and Transformation

Hemp, particularly products containing CBD, can support Scorpio individuals by promoting deep healing, reducing anxiety, and enhancing their ability to navigate transformation. Here are some ways hemp can help Scorpio harness their strengths and address their challenges:

- **Promoting Deep Healing**: Scorpio's intense emotional nature can benefit from the calming and healing effects of CBD. Using CBD can help reduce stress and promote a sense of inner peace, allowing Scorpio to heal from past traumas and emotional wounds.
- **Reducing Anxiety**: Scorpio's tendency to feel deeply can lead to anxiety. CBD's anxiolytic properties can help reduce anxiety and promote a sense of calm, allowing Scorpio to approach situations with a clear and composed mind.
- **Enhancing Transformation**: Scorpios thrive on transformation and change. CBD can help stabilize mood and promote emotional balance, allowing Scorpio to navigate their transformative journeys with greater ease and resilience.
- **Supporting Emotional Balance**: Emotional stability is crucial for Scorpio to manage their intensity and obsessive tendencies. CBD can help regulate mood and promote emotional balance, allowing Scorpio to maintain healthy relationships and achieve their goals without becoming overwhelmed.
- **Improving Sleep Quality**: Adequate rest is essential for Scorpio to recharge their energy and maintain their resilience. CBD can help improve sleep quality by promoting relaxation and reducing insomnia. Using CBD before bedtime can help Scorpio achieve restful sleep and wake up feeling refreshed.

Rituals and Practices for Scorpio Individuals

To harness their transformative qualities and maintain balance, Scorpio individuals can incorporate the following rituals and practices into their routine:

Morning Routine

- **CBD-Infused Breakfast**: Start the day with a CBD-infused breakfast to promote deep healing and set a positive tone for the day. Add CBD oil to a smoothie or enjoy a CBD-infused granola bar. This can help Scorpio maintain their energy and mental clarity throughout the day.

Mindfulness and Meditation

- **Guided Meditation**: Practice guided meditation to promote relaxation and mental clarity. Use CBD to enhance relaxation and focus. Find a quiet space, sit comfortably, and listen to a guided meditation that focuses on deep healing and transformation.
- **Breathwork Exercises**: Engage in breathwork exercises to calm the mind and reduce anxiety. Practice deep, intentional breathing to improve focus and emotional regulation. Use CBD to enhance relaxation during breathwork sessions.

Creative Expression

- **Art and Journaling**: Engage in creative projects like painting, drawing, or writing to express emotions and ideas. Use CBD to reduce anxiety and enhance creative flow. Allow your intuition to guide your artistic process and enjoy the satisfaction of creating something meaningful.
- **Shadow Work**: Scorpio's transformative nature makes them well-suited for shadow work. Use CBD to promote relaxation and reduce anxiety while exploring the hidden aspects of the psyche. Reflect on past experiences, fears, and desires, and integrate these insights into your personal growth journey.

Health and Wellness

- **Healthy Eating**: Practice mindful eating to nourish the body and mind. Choose nutritious, whole foods and savor each bite. Use CBD to promote relaxation and enhance the mindful eating experience.

- **Exercise Routine:** Incorporate regular physical exercise into the routine to promote physical health and emotional well-being. Use CBD to alleviate muscle soreness and enhance relaxation after workouts.

Goal Setting and Planning

- **Task Management:** Set specific, measurable goals and track progress regularly. Use a planner or digital tool to stay organized and motivated. Incorporate CBD into the routine to maintain focus and reduce stress while working towards goals.
- **Vision Boarding:** Create a vision board to visualize goals and aspirations. Use images, quotes, and symbols that resonate with Scorpio's desire for transformation and deep healing. Place the vision board in a prominent location as a daily reminder of their path. Use CBD to promote relaxation and focus while creating the vision board.

Social Engagement

- **Hosting Gatherings:** Scorpios enjoy creating intimate and meaningful environments for their loved ones. Host gatherings with friends and family, incorporating CBD-infused foods and drinks. Create a relaxing and inviting atmosphere for your guests to enjoy deep conversations and connections.
- **Joining Clubs and Groups:** Engage in social clubs or interest groups that align with Scorpio's passions. Use CBD to manage social anxiety and enhance positive interactions. Participate in group activities and enjoy the sense of community and connection.

Personal Development

- **Positive Affirmations**: Practice positive affirmations to reinforce confidence and emotional balance. Write down affirmations like "I am strong and resilient" or "I embrace transformation with grace." Repeat these affirmations daily to cultivate a positive mindset.
- **Conflict Resolution**: Develop conflict resolution skills to manage Scorpio's intensity and need for control. Use CBD to promote calm and focus during difficult conversations. Practice active listening, empathy, and assertive communication to resolve conflicts constructively.

Self-Care and Relaxation

- **Spa Day at Home**: Create a spa day at home using CBD-infused products. Enjoy a facial mask, body scrub, and relaxing bath. Use CBD lotions and oils for self-massage. This practice can help Scorpio feel pampered and rejuvenated.
- **Relaxing Bath Ritual**: Create a relaxing bath ritual using CBD-infused bath bombs or salts. Add calming essential oils like lavender or patchouli. Light candles and play soothing music to enhance the sensory experience. Soak in the warm water, letting go of stress and tension.

Learning and Exploration

- **Continual Learning**: Embrace Scorpio's love for knowledge and personal growth by continually learning new skills or exploring new interests. Take classes, attend workshops, or engage in self-directed learning. Use CBD to enhance focus and reduce stress during the learning process.
- **Travel and Adventure**: Plan adventures or travel experiences that align with Scorpio's love for transformation and new experiences.

Use CBD to manage travel-related stress and enhance enjoyment. Reflect on the lessons and insights gained from these experiences.

Community Engagement

- **Volunteering and Service**: Engage in volunteer work or community service projects. Use CBD to manage stress and maintain emotional balance while helping others. Reflect on the sense of fulfillment and connection gained from giving back.
- **Public Speaking and Networking**: Scorpio's strategic and investigative skills can be honed through public speaking and networking events. Use CBD to reduce anxiety and enhance confidence. Practice speeches, engage in discussions, and build connections within your community.

Emotional and Physical Health

- **Yoga and Physical Exercise**: Incorporate physical exercise, such as yoga, into the routine to promote physical health and emotional well-being. Use CBD to alleviate muscle soreness and enhance relaxation after workouts.
- **Health Checkups**: Regular health checkups and wellness routines can help Scorpio stay on top of their physical health. Use CBD to reduce anxiety related to medical appointments and promote overall well-being.

In this chapter, we have explored the characteristics and traits of Scorpio, the benefits of using hemp to support their deep healing and transformation, and various rituals and practices to enhance their transformative nature. By understanding the intense and resilient nature of Scorpio and incorporating hemp products into their routine, Scorpio individuals can harness their strengths, balance their challenges, and achieve personal and professional growth. As we continue our journey through this book, we will discover more ways to integrate hemp and astrology for holistic healing and personal development.

Check out my Virtual dispensary for all your hemp needs: https://shift.store/sg1fan23477/retail

Chapter 33: Sagittarius: The Explorer
Characteristics and Traits of Sagittarius

Sagittarius, the ninth sign of the zodiac, is known for its adventurous spirit and quest for knowledge. Ruled by Jupiter, the planet of expansion, luck, and wisdom, Sagittarius embodies optimism, freedom, and a love for exploration. This mutable fire sign is often seen as enthusiastic, philosophical, and open-minded, with a natural ability to inspire others and seek out new experiences.

- **Positive Traits:**
  - **Adventurous**: Sagittarius individuals have a strong desire to explore the world and experience new things. They thrive on adventure and are always looking for their next big journey.
  - **Optimistic**: With their positive outlook on life, Sagittarians are often seen as cheerful and hopeful. They believe in the best possible outcomes and inspire others with their enthusiasm.
  - **Philosophical**: Sagittarius has a deep love for learning and understanding. They enjoy pondering life's big questions and exploring different philosophies and belief systems.
  - **Independent**: Valuing their freedom, Sagittarians are fiercely independent. They prefer to chart their own course and resist being tied down.
  - **Generous**: Known for their generosity, Sagittarians are willing to share their knowledge, experiences, and resources with others.
- **Challenges:**

- **Impatient**: Sagittarius's desire for new experiences can lead to impatience. They may struggle with waiting and become frustrated with delays.
- **Blunt**: Known for their honesty, Sagittarians can sometimes be overly blunt. Their direct communication style can come across as tactless or insensitive.
- **Restless**: With their constant need for movement and change, Sagittarians can become easily bored and restless. They may have difficulty sticking to long-term projects.
- **Overconfident**: Sagittarius's optimism can sometimes lead to overconfidence. They may take risks without fully considering the consequences.
- **Irresponsible**: In their quest for freedom, Sagittarians may sometimes shirk responsibilities. They may struggle with commitments and prefer to live in the moment.

- **Sagittarius in Relationships**: In relationships, Sagittarius is playful, adventurous, and enthusiastic. They bring excitement and a sense of discovery to their partnerships but may need to work on being more sensitive and responsible. They value intellectual and philosophical connections and seek partners who share their love for adventure and learning.
- **Sagittarius in Career**: Professionally, Sagittarius excels in roles that require exploration, education, and inspiration. They thrive in careers related to travel, teaching, writing, and public speaking. Their ability to see the big picture and inspire others makes them valuable in any role that involves vision and expansion.

Hemp for Sagittarius: Adventure and Wisdom

Hemp, particularly products containing CBD, can support Sagittarius individuals by enhancing their sense of adventure, promoting relaxation, and aiding in their quest for wisdom. Here are some ways hemp can help Sagittarius harness their strengths and address their challenges:

- **Enhancing Adventure**: Sagittarius's love for adventure can be enhanced with the calming effects of CBD, which can help reduce anxiety and promote relaxation, allowing them to fully enjoy their explorations. Using CBD can help Sagittarians remain calm and focused during their travels and new experiences.
- **Promoting Relaxation**: Sagittarius's restless nature can benefit from CBD's calming properties. CBD can help reduce stress and promote a sense of tranquility, allowing Sagittarius to unwind and recharge after their adventures.
- **Supporting Wisdom**: Sagittarians have a thirst for knowledge and wisdom. CBD can enhance focus and mental clarity, making it easier for Sagittarius to engage in deep learning and philosophical exploration. Incorporating CBD into their daily routine can support their intellectual pursuits.
- **Improving Sleep Quality**: Adequate rest is crucial for Sagittarius to maintain their energy and enthusiasm. CBD can help improve sleep quality by promoting relaxation and reducing insomnia. Using CBD before bedtime can help Sagittarius achieve restful sleep and wake up feeling refreshed.
- **Alleviating Physical Discomfort**: The physically active lifestyle of Sagittarius can lead to muscle soreness and discomfort. CBD topicals, such as balms and creams, can help alleviate pain and inflammation, allowing Sagittarius to stay active and enjoy their adventures without physical limitations.

Rituals and Practices for Sagittarius Individuals

To harness their exploratory nature and maintain balance, Sagittarius individuals can incorporate the following rituals and practices into their routine:

Morning Routine

- **CBD-Infused Breakfast**: Start the day with a CBD-infused breakfast to promote adventure and wisdom. Add CBD oil to a smoothie or enjoy a CBD-infused granola bar. This can help Sagittarius maintain their energy and mental clarity throughout the day.

Mindfulness and Meditation

- **Guided Meditation**: Practice guided meditation to promote relaxation and mental clarity. Use CBD to enhance relaxation and focus. Find a quiet space, sit comfortably, and listen to a guided meditation that focuses on exploration and inner wisdom.
- **Breathwork Exercises**: Engage in breathwork exercises to calm the mind and reduce anxiety. Practice deep, intentional breathing to improve focus and emotional regulation. Use CBD to enhance relaxation during breathwork sessions.

Creative Expression

- **Journaling and Writing**: Keep a journal to reflect on experiences, thoughts, and ideas. Use a hemp journal and CBD to promote relaxation and clarity while writing. Reflect on personal growth, set intentions, and explore new ideas. Writing travel stories or philosophical musings can be particularly fulfilling for Sagittarius.
- **Art and Craft Projects**: Engage in creative projects like painting, drawing, or crafting to express emotions and ideas. Use CBD to reduce anxiety and enhance creative flow. Allow your intuition to guide your artistic process and enjoy the satisfaction of creating something meaningful.

Health and Wellness

- **Healthy Eating**: Practice mindful eating to nourish the body and mind. Choose nutritious, whole foods and savor each bite.

Use CBD to promote relaxation and enhance the mindful eating experience.

- **Exercise Routine**: Incorporate regular physical exercise into the routine to promote physical health and emotional well-being. Use CBD to alleviate muscle soreness and enhance relaxation after workouts. Outdoor activities such as hiking, biking, or swimming can be particularly enjoyable for Sagittarius.

Goal Setting and Planning

- **Task Management**: Set specific, measurable goals and track progress regularly. Use a planner or digital tool to stay organized and motivated. Incorporate CBD into the routine to maintain focus and reduce stress while working towards goals.
- **Vision Boarding**: Create a vision board to visualize goals and aspirations. Use images, quotes, and symbols that resonate with Sagittarius's desire for adventure and wisdom. Place the vision board in a prominent location as a daily reminder of their path. Use CBD to promote relaxation and focus while creating the vision board.

Social Engagement

- **Hosting Gatherings**: Sagittarians enjoy socializing and creating vibrant environments for their loved ones. Host gatherings with friends and family, incorporating CBD-infused foods and drinks. Create a fun and inviting atmosphere for your guests to enjoy stimulating conversations and activities.
- **Joining Clubs and Groups**: Engage in social clubs or interest groups that align with Sagittarius's passions. Use CBD to manage social anxiety and enhance positive interactions. Participate in group activities and enjoy the sense of community and connection.

Personal Development

- **Positive Affirmations**: Practice positive affirmations to reinforce confidence and emotional balance. Write down affirmations like "I am open to new experiences and learning" or "I embrace adventure with courage." Repeat these affirmations daily to cultivate a positive mindset.
- **Conflict Resolution**: Develop conflict resolution skills to manage Sagittarius's bluntness and impatience. Use CBD to promote calm and focus during difficult conversations. Practice active listening, empathy, and assertive communication to resolve conflicts constructively.

Self-Care and Relaxation

- **Spa Day at Home**: Create a spa day at home using CBD-infused products. Enjoy a facial mask, body scrub, and relaxing bath. Use CBD lotions and oils for self-massage. This practice can help Sagittarius feel pampered and rejuvenated.
- **Relaxing Bath Ritual**: Create a relaxing bath ritual using CBD-infused bath bombs or salts. Add calming essential oils like lavender or eucalyptus. Light candles and play soothing music to enhance the sensory experience. Soak in the warm water, letting go of stress and tension.

Learning and Exploration

- **Continual Learning**: Embrace Sagittarius's love for knowledge and personal growth by continually learning new skills or exploring new interests. Take classes, attend workshops, or engage in self-directed learning. Use CBD to enhance focus and reduce stress during the learning process.

- **Travel and Adventure**: Plan adventures or travel experiences that align with Sagittarius's love for exploration and new experiences. Use CBD to manage travel-related stress and enhance enjoyment. Reflect on the lessons and insights gained from these experiences.

Community Engagement

- **Volunteering and Service**: Engage in volunteer work or community service projects. Use CBD to manage stress and maintain emotional balance while helping others. Reflect on the sense of fulfillment and connection gained from giving back.
- **Public Speaking and Networking**: Sagittarius's communication and inspirational skills can be honed through public speaking and networking events. Use CBD to reduce anxiety and enhance confidence. Practice speeches, engage in discussions, and build connections within your community.

Emotional and Physical Health

- **Yoga and Physical Exercise**: Incorporate physical exercise, such as yoga, into the routine to promote physical health and emotional well-being. Use CBD to alleviate muscle soreness and enhance relaxation after workouts.
- **Health Checkups**: Regular health checkups and wellness routines can help Sagittarius stay on top of their physical health. Use CBD to reduce anxiety related to medical appointments and promote overall well-being.

In this chapter, we have explored the characteristics and traits of Sagittarius, the benefits of using hemp to support their adventure and wisdom, and various rituals and practices to enhance their exploratory nature. By understanding the enthusiastic and philosophical nature of Sagittarius and incorporating hemp products into their routine,

Sagittarius individuals can harness their strengths, balance their challenges, and achieve personal and professional growth. As we continue our journey through this book, we will discover more ways to integrate hemp and astrology for holistic healing and personal development.

Check out my Virtual dispensary for all your hemp needs: https://shift.store/sg1fan23477/retail

Chapter 34: Capricorn: The Achiever
Characteristics and Traits of Capricorn

Capricorn, the tenth sign of the zodiac, is known for its ambitious and disciplined nature. Ruled by Saturn, the planet of structure, responsibility, and discipline, Capricorn embodies practicality, determination, and a strong desire for achievement. This cardinal earth sign is often seen as reliable, hardworking, and strategic, with a natural ability to set and accomplish long-term goals.

- **Positive Traits:**
  - **Ambitious**: Capricorns are highly driven and goal-oriented. They have a strong desire to succeed and are willing to put in the hard work to achieve their aspirations.
  - **Disciplined**: With their innate sense of discipline, Capricorns excel in creating and sticking to plans. They are persistent and have excellent self-control.
  - **Practical**: Capricorns are grounded in reality and prefer practical solutions. They are skilled at problem-solving and making sound decisions based on logic and reason.
  - **Responsible**: Capricorns take their responsibilities seriously and are reliable and dependable. They are often the ones others turn to in times of need.
  - **Strategic**: Capricorns have a strategic mind and excel in planning and organizing. They are adept at seeing the big picture and making long-term plans.
- **Challenges:**
  - **Pessimistic**: Capricorn's realistic nature can sometimes turn into pessimism. They may focus on potential problems and obstacles, leading to a negative outlook.

- **Stubborn**: As a cardinal sign, Capricorns can be stubborn and resistant to change. They may struggle to adapt to new situations or perspectives.
- **Workaholic**: Capricorns' strong work ethic can sometimes lead to workaholism. They may prioritize work over rest and relaxation, leading to burnout.
- **Aloof**: Capricorns can be reserved and distant. They may struggle to express their emotions and connect with others on a deeper level.
- **Overly Serious**: Capricorns' focus on responsibility and achievement can make them overly serious. They may need to work on finding balance and allowing themselves to enjoy life's lighter moments.

- **Capricorn in Relationships**: In relationships, Capricorn is loyal, supportive, and committed. They bring stability and reliability to their partnerships but may need to work on being more emotionally open and flexible. They value intellectual and practical connections and seek partners who share their dedication and ambition.
- **Capricorn in Career**: Professionally, Capricorn excels in roles that require discipline, organization, and strategic thinking. They thrive in careers related to business, finance, law, and management. Their ability to set goals and work diligently towards them makes them valuable in any role that involves long-term planning and achievement.

Hemp for Capricorn: Discipline and Ambition

Hemp, particularly products containing CBD, can support Capricorn individuals by enhancing their discipline, reducing stress, and promoting overall well-being. Here are some ways hemp can help Capricorn harness their strengths and address their challenges:

- **Enhancing Discipline**: Capricorn's disciplined nature can be further supported with the calming and balancing effects of CBD. Using CBD can help reduce stress and promote focus, allowing Capricorns to stick to their plans and achieve their goals with greater ease.
- **Reducing Stress**: Capricorn's ambitious and hardworking nature can lead to stress and burnout. CBD's anxiolytic properties can help reduce stress and promote relaxation, allowing Capricorns to unwind and recharge after a long day.
- **Supporting Emotional Balance**: Emotional stability is crucial for Capricorn to manage their pessimism and aloofness. CBD can help regulate mood and promote emotional balance, allowing Capricorn to connect with others and maintain a positive outlook.
- **Improving Sleep Quality**: Adequate rest is essential for Capricorn to maintain their energy and productivity. CBD can help improve sleep quality by promoting relaxation and reducing insomnia. Using CBD before bedtime can help Capricorn achieve restful sleep and wake up feeling refreshed.
- **Alleviating Physical Discomfort**: The physically demanding nature of Capricorn's work ethic can lead to muscle soreness and discomfort. CBD topicals, such as balms and creams, can help alleviate pain and inflammation, allowing Capricorn to stay active and productive without physical limitations.

Rituals and Practices for Capricorn Individuals

To harness their ambitious nature and maintain balance, Capricorn individuals can incorporate the following rituals and practices into their routine:

Morning Routine

- **CBD-Infused Breakfast**: Start the day with a CBD-infused breakfast to promote discipline and set a positive tone for the day.

Add CBD oil to a smoothie or enjoy a CBD-infused granola bar. This can help Capricorn maintain their energy and mental clarity throughout the day.

Mindfulness and Meditation

- **Guided Meditation**: Practice guided meditation to promote relaxation and mental clarity. Use CBD to enhance relaxation and focus. Find a quiet space, sit comfortably, and listen to a guided meditation that focuses on discipline and ambition.
- **Breathwork Exercises**: Engage in breathwork exercises to calm the mind and reduce anxiety. Practice deep, intentional breathing to improve focus and emotional regulation. Use CBD to enhance relaxation during breathwork sessions.

Creative Expression

- **Journaling and Planning**: Keep a journal to reflect on experiences, thoughts, and goals. Use a hemp journal and CBD to promote relaxation and clarity while writing. Reflect on personal growth, set intentions, and plan your path to achieving your goals.
- **Art and Craft Projects**: Engage in creative projects like painting, drawing, or crafting to express emotions and ideas. Use CBD to reduce anxiety and enhance creative flow. Allow your intuition to guide your artistic process and enjoy the satisfaction of creating something meaningful.

Health and Wellness

- **Healthy Eating**: Practice mindful eating to nourish the body and mind. Choose nutritious, whole foods and savor each bite.

Use CBD to promote relaxation and enhance the mindful eating experience.

- **Exercise Routine**: Incorporate regular physical exercise into the routine to promote physical health and emotional well-being. Use CBD to alleviate muscle soreness and enhance relaxation after workouts. Activities like weightlifting, running, or yoga can be particularly beneficial for Capricorn.

Goal Setting and Planning

- **Task Management**: Set specific, measurable goals and track progress regularly. Use a planner or digital tool to stay organized and motivated. Incorporate CBD into the routine to maintain focus and reduce stress while working towards goals.
- **Vision Boarding**: Create a vision board to visualize goals and aspirations. Use images, quotes, and symbols that resonate with Capricorn's desire for achievement and discipline. Place the vision board in a prominent location as a daily reminder of their path. Use CBD to promote relaxation and focus while creating the vision board.

Social Engagement

- **Hosting Gatherings**: Capricorns enjoy creating organized and welcoming environments for their loved ones. Host gatherings with friends and family, incorporating CBD-infused foods and drinks. Create a relaxing and inviting atmosphere for your guests to enjoy.
- **Joining Clubs and Groups**: Engage in social clubs or interest groups that align with Capricorn's passions. Use CBD to manage social anxiety and enhance positive interactions. Participate in group activities and enjoy the sense of community and connection.

Personal Development

- **Positive Affirmations**: Practice positive affirmations to reinforce confidence and emotional balance. Write down affirmations like "I am disciplined and determined" or "I achieve my goals with perseverance." Repeat these affirmations daily to cultivate a positive mindset.
- **Conflict Resolution**: Develop conflict resolution skills to manage Capricorn's stubbornness and pessimism. Use CBD to promote calm and focus during difficult conversations. Practice active listening, empathy, and assertive communication to resolve conflicts constructively.

Self-Care and Relaxation

- **Spa Day at Home**: Create a spa day at home using CBD-infused products. Enjoy a facial mask, body scrub, and relaxing bath. Use CBD lotions and oils for self-massage. This practice can help Capricorn feel pampered and rejuvenated.
- **Relaxing Bath Ritual**: Create a relaxing bath ritual using CBD-infused bath bombs or salts. Add calming essential oils like lavender or eucalyptus. Light candles and play soothing music to enhance the sensory experience. Soak in the warm water, letting go of stress and tension.

Learning and Exploration

- **Continual Learning**: Embrace Capricorn's love for knowledge and personal growth by continually learning new skills or exploring new interests. Take classes, attend workshops, or engage in self-directed learning. Use CBD to enhance focus and reduce stress during the learning process.

- **Travel and Adventure**: Plan adventures or travel experiences that align with Capricorn's love for structure and new experiences. Use CBD to manage travel-related stress and enhance enjoyment. Reflect on the lessons and insights gained from these experiences.

Community Engagement

- **Volunteering and Service**: Engage in volunteer work or community service projects. Use CBD to manage stress and maintain emotional balance while helping others. Reflect on the sense of fulfillment and connection gained from giving back.
- **Public Speaking and Networking**: Capricorn's strategic and disciplined skills can be honed through public speaking and networking events. Use CBD to reduce anxiety and enhance confidence. Practice speeches, engage in discussions, and build connections within your community.

Emotional and Physical Health

- **Yoga and Physical Exercise**: Incorporate physical exercise, such as yoga, into the routine to promote physical health and emotional well-being. Use CBD to alleviate muscle soreness and enhance relaxation after workouts.
- **Health Checkups**: Regular health checkups and wellness routines can help Capricorn stay on top of their physical health. Use CBD to reduce anxiety related to medical appointments and promote overall well-being.

In this chapter, we have explored the characteristics and traits of Capricorn, the benefits of using hemp to support their discipline and ambition, and various rituals and practices to enhance their achieving nature. By understanding the ambitious and practical nature of Capricorn and incorporating hemp products into their routine, Capricorn individuals can harness their strengths, balance their challenges, and achieve personal and professional growth. As we continue our journey through this book, we will discover more ways to integrate hemp and astrology for holistic healing and personal development.

Check out my Virtual dispensary for all your hemp needs: https://shift.store/sg1fan23477/retail

Chapter 35: Aquarius: The Visionary
Characteristics and Traits of Aquarius

Aquarius, the eleventh sign of the zodiac, is known for its forward-thinking and humanitarian nature. Ruled by Uranus, the planet of innovation and sudden change, and traditionally by Saturn, the planet of structure and discipline, Aquarius embodies originality, intellectualism, and a strong desire for social progress. This fixed air sign is often seen as independent, unconventional, and visionary, with a natural ability to think outside the box and inspire change.

- **Positive Traits:**
  - **Innovative**: Aquarians are natural innovators and thinkers. They have a knack for coming up with original ideas and solutions and are often ahead of their time.
  - **Humanitarian**: With a deep sense of social justice, Aquarians are committed to making the world a better place. They are passionate about humanitarian causes and often work towards social progress.
  - **Intellectual**: Aquarius individuals have a strong intellectual curiosity. They enjoy exploring new ideas, engaging in thought-provoking discussions, and expanding their knowledge.
  - **Independent**: Valuing their freedom, Aquarians are fiercely independent. They prefer to think and act for themselves and resist conformity.
  - **Visionary**: Aquarians are forward-thinking and have a clear vision for the future. They are often driven by a desire to bring about positive change and innovation.
- **Challenges:**
  - **Detached**: Aquarius's intellectual nature can sometimes make them appear detached or aloof. They may struggle

with expressing their emotions and connecting with others on a deeper level.

- **Stubborn**: As a fixed sign, Aquarians can be stubborn and resistant to change. They may hold firmly to their ideas and beliefs, even when faced with new information.
- **Unpredictable**: Ruled by Uranus, Aquarians can be unpredictable and erratic. They may change their minds or actions suddenly, which can be confusing to others.
- **Aloof**: Aquarians' need for independence can sometimes make them seem distant or unapproachable. They may need to work on being more emotionally available.
- **Overly Idealistic**: Aquarians' visionary nature can sometimes lead to overly idealistic thinking. They may have unrealistic expectations and struggle with practical implementation.

- **Aquarius in Relationships**: In relationships, Aquarius is open-minded, intellectually stimulating, and supportive. They bring excitement and a sense of adventure to their partnerships but may need to work on being more emotionally available and consistent. They value intellectual connections and seek partners who share their passion for ideas and social progress.
- **Aquarius in Career**: Professionally, Aquarius excels in roles that require innovation, creativity, and intellectual rigor. They thrive in careers related to technology, science, research, social activism, and the arts. Their ability to think outside the box and drive change makes them valuable in any role that involves progress and innovation.

Hemp for Aquarius: Innovation and Humanitarianism

Hemp, particularly products containing CBD, can support Aquarius individuals by enhancing their creativity, reducing stress, and promoting overall well-being. Here are some ways hemp can help Aquarius harness their strengths and address their challenges:

- **Enhancing Creativity**: Aquarius's innovative nature can be further supported with the calming and balancing effects of CBD. Using CBD can help reduce mental fog and enhance focus, allowing Aquarians to channel their creative energy more effectively.
- **Reducing Stress**: Aquarius's humanitarian efforts and intellectual pursuits can lead to stress and mental fatigue. CBD's anxiolytic properties can help reduce stress and promote relaxation, allowing Aquarians to unwind and recharge after a long day.
- **Supporting Emotional Balance**: Emotional stability is crucial for Aquarius to manage their detachment and unpredictability. CBD can help regulate mood and promote emotional balance, allowing Aquarius to connect with others and maintain a positive outlook.
- **Improving Sleep Quality**: Adequate rest is essential for Aquarius to maintain their energy and mental clarity. CBD can help improve sleep quality by promoting relaxation and reducing insomnia. Using CBD before bedtime can help Aquarius achieve restful sleep and wake up feeling refreshed.
- **Alleviating Physical Discomfort**: The mentally demanding nature of Aquarius's pursuits can lead to physical tension and discomfort. CBD topicals, such as balms and creams, can help alleviate pain and inflammation, allowing Aquarius to stay active and productive without physical limitations.

Rituals and Practices for Aquarius Individuals

To harness their visionary nature and maintain balance, Aquarius individuals can incorporate the following rituals and practices into their routine:

Morning Routine

- **CBD-Infused Breakfast**: Start the day with a CBD-infused breakfast to promote innovation and set a positive tone for the day. Add CBD oil to a smoothie or enjoy a CBD-infused granola bar. This can help Aquarius maintain their energy and mental clarity throughout the day.

Mindfulness and Meditation

- **Guided Meditation**: Practice guided meditation to promote relaxation and mental clarity. Use CBD to enhance relaxation and focus. Find a quiet space, sit comfortably, and listen to a guided meditation that focuses on creativity and visionary thinking.
- **Breathwork Exercises**: Engage in breathwork exercises to calm the mind and reduce anxiety. Practice deep, intentional breathing to improve focus and emotional regulation. Use CBD to enhance relaxation during breathwork sessions.

Creative Expression

- **Journaling and Writing**: Keep a journal to reflect on experiences, thoughts, and ideas. Use a hemp journal and CBD to promote relaxation and clarity while writing. Reflect on personal growth, set intentions, and explore new ideas. Writing about future visions or social innovations can be particularly fulfilling for Aquarius.
- **Art and Craft Projects**: Engage in creative projects like painting, drawing, or crafting to express emotions and ideas. Use CBD to reduce anxiety and enhance creative flow. Allow your intuition to guide your artistic process and enjoy the satisfaction of creating something meaningful.

Health and Wellness

- **Healthy Eating**: Practice mindful eating to nourish the body and mind. Choose nutritious, whole foods and savor each bite.

Use CBD to promote relaxation and enhance the mindful eating experience.

- **Exercise Routine**: Incorporate regular physical exercise into the routine to promote physical health and emotional well-being. Use CBD to alleviate muscle soreness and enhance relaxation after workouts. Activities like running, cycling, or group sports can be particularly beneficial for Aquarius.

Goal Setting and Planning

- **Task Management**: Set specific, measurable goals and track progress regularly. Use a planner or digital tool to stay organized and motivated. Incorporate CBD into the routine to maintain focus and reduce stress while working towards goals.
- **Vision Boarding**: Create a vision board to visualize goals and aspirations. Use images, quotes, and symbols that resonate with Aquarius's desire for innovation and humanitarianism. Place the vision board in a prominent location as a daily reminder of their path. Use CBD to promote relaxation and focus while creating the vision board.

Social Engagement

- **Hosting Gatherings**: Aquarians enjoy socializing and creating vibrant environments for their loved ones. Host gatherings with friends and family, incorporating CBD-infused foods and drinks. Create a fun and inviting atmosphere for your guests to enjoy stimulating conversations and activities.
- **Joining Clubs and Groups**: Engage in social clubs or interest groups that align with Aquarius's passions. Use CBD to manage social anxiety and enhance positive interactions. Participate in group activities and enjoy the sense of community and connection.

Personal Development

- **Positive Affirmations**: Practice positive affirmations to reinforce confidence and emotional balance. Write down affirmations like "I am innovative and visionary" or "I embrace change and inspire progress." Repeat these affirmations daily to cultivate a positive mindset.
- **Conflict Resolution**: Develop conflict resolution skills to manage Aquarius's detachment and unpredictability. Use CBD to promote calm and focus during difficult conversations. Practice active listening, empathy, and assertive communication to resolve conflicts constructively.

Self-Care and Relaxation

- **Spa Day at Home**: Create a spa day at home using CBD-infused products. Enjoy a facial mask, body scrub, and relaxing bath. Use CBD lotions and oils for self-massage. This practice can help Aquarius feel pampered and rejuvenated.
- **Relaxing Bath Ritual**: Create a relaxing bath ritual using CBD-infused bath bombs or salts. Add calming essential oils like lavender or eucalyptus. Light candles and play soothing music to enhance the sensory experience. Soak in the warm water, letting go of stress and tension.

Learning and Exploration

- **Continual Learning**: Embrace Aquarius's love for knowledge and personal growth by continually learning new skills or exploring new interests. Take classes, attend workshops, or engage in self-directed learning. Use CBD to enhance focus and reduce stress during the learning process.

- **Travel and Adventure:** Plan adventures or travel experiences that align with Aquarius's love for exploration and new experiences. Use CBD to manage travel-related stress and enhance enjoyment. Reflect on the lessons and insights gained from these experiences.

Community Engagement

- **Volunteering and Service:** Engage in volunteer work or community service projects. Use CBD to manage stress and maintain emotional balance while helping others. Reflect on the sense of fulfillment and connection gained from giving back.
- **Public Speaking and Networking:** Aquarius's communication and inspirational skills can be honed through public speaking and networking events. Use CBD to reduce anxiety and enhance confidence. Practice speeches, engage in discussions, and build connections within your community.

Emotional and Physical Health

- **Yoga and Physical Exercise:** Incorporate physical exercise, such as yoga, into the routine to promote physical health and emotional well-being. Use CBD to alleviate muscle soreness and enhance relaxation after workouts.
- **Health Checkups:** Regular health checkups and wellness routines can help Aquarius stay on top of their physical health. Use CBD to reduce anxiety related to medical appointments and promote overall well-being.

In this chapter, we have explored the characteristics and traits of Aquarius, the benefits of using hemp to support their innovation and humanitarianism, and various rituals and practices to enhance their visionary nature. By understanding the independent and forward-thinking nature of Aquarius and incorporating hemp products into their routine, Aquarius individuals can harness their strengths, balance their challenges, and achieve personal and professional growth. As we continue our journey through this book, we will discover more ways to integrate hemp and astrology for holistic healing and personal development.

Check out my Virtual dispensary for all your hemp needs: https://shift.store/sg1fan23477/retail

Chapter 36: Pisces: The Dreamer
Characteristics and Traits of Pisces

Pisces, the twelfth and final sign of the zodiac, is known for its dreamy, intuitive, and empathetic nature. Ruled by Neptune, the planet of illusion, dreams, and spirituality, and traditionally by Jupiter, the planet of expansion and wisdom, Pisces embodies creativity, sensitivity, and a deep connection to the spiritual realm. This mutable water sign is often seen as compassionate, artistic, and selfless, with a natural ability to understand and empathize with others.

- **Positive Traits:**
  - **Intuitive**: Pisceans have a strong sense of intuition and are highly perceptive. They often have an uncanny ability to sense what others are feeling and thinking.
  - **Empathetic**: Pisces individuals are deeply empathetic and compassionate. They are able to connect with others on an emotional level and provide comfort and support.
  - **Creative**: With their vivid imagination and artistic flair, Pisceans excel in creative endeavors. They have a natural talent for the arts, music, and writing.
  - **Spiritual**: Pisces is deeply connected to the spiritual realm. They are often drawn to mysticism, meditation, and exploring the deeper meanings of life.
  - **Selfless**: Pisceans are known for their selfless nature. They are often willing to put others' needs before their own and are dedicated to helping those in need.
- **Challenges:**
  - **Escapist**: Pisces's tendency to dream can sometimes lead to escapism. They may struggle to face reality and seek refuge in fantasies or addictive behaviors.

- ○ **Overly Sensitive**: Pisceans' deep empathy can make them overly sensitive. They may be easily hurt by the actions and words of others and struggle to set boundaries.
  - ○ **Indecisive**: Pisces's mutable nature can lead to indecisiveness. They may have difficulty making decisions and can be easily influenced by others.
  - ○ **Idealistic**: Pisceans' idealism can sometimes result in unrealistic expectations. They may struggle to accept imperfections in themselves and others.
  - ○ **Self-Sacrificing**: While their selflessness is a strength, it can also be a challenge. Pisceans may neglect their own needs and well-being in their efforts to help others.
- **Pisces in Relationships**: In relationships, Pisces is loving, romantic, and deeply committed. They bring warmth and emotional depth to their partnerships but may need to work on setting boundaries and managing their sensitivity. They value emotional and spiritual connections and seek partners who appreciate their compassion and creativity.
- **Pisces in Career**: Professionally, Pisces excels in roles that require creativity, empathy, and intuition. They thrive in careers related to the arts, healing professions, social work, and spiritual guidance. Their ability to connect with others and bring imaginative solutions makes them valuable in any role that involves emotional intelligence and creativity.

Hemp for Pisces: Intuition and Empathy

Hemp, particularly products containing CBD, can support Pisces individuals by enhancing their intuition, reducing anxiety, and promoting overall well-being. Here are some ways hemp can help Pisces harness their strengths and address their challenges:

- **Enhancing Intuition**: Pisces's intuitive nature can be further supported with the calming and balancing effects of CBD. Using

CBD can help reduce mental fog and enhance focus, allowing Pisceans to trust and follow their intuitive insights more effectively.

- **Reducing Anxiety**: Pisces's sensitivity and empathy can lead to anxiety and emotional overwhelm. CBD's anxiolytic properties can help reduce anxiety and promote relaxation, allowing Pisceans to navigate their emotions with greater ease.

- **Supporting Emotional Balance**: Emotional stability is crucial for Pisces to manage their sensitivity and escapist tendencies. CBD can help regulate mood and promote emotional balance, allowing Pisces to maintain healthy relationships and achieve their goals without becoming overwhelmed.

- **Improving Sleep Quality**: Adequate rest is essential for Pisces to recharge their energy and maintain their creative and empathetic abilities. CBD can help improve sleep quality by promoting relaxation and reducing insomnia. Using CBD before bedtime can help Pisces achieve restful sleep and wake up feeling refreshed.

- **Alleviating Physical Discomfort**: The emotionally demanding nature of Pisces's pursuits can lead to physical tension and discomfort. CBD topicals, such as balms and creams, can help alleviate pain and inflammation, allowing Pisces to stay active and engaged without physical limitations.

Rituals and Practices for Pisces Individual

To harness their dreamy nature and maintain balance, Pisces individuals can incorporate the following rituals and practices into their routine:

Morning Routine

- **CBD-Infused Breakfast**: Start the day with a CBD-infused breakfast to promote intuition and set a positive tone for the day. Add CBD oil to a smoothie or enjoy a CBD-infused granola bar. This can help Pisces maintain their energy and mental clarity throughout the day.

Mindfulness and Meditation

- **Guided Meditation**: Practice guided meditation to promote relaxation and mental clarity. Use CBD to enhance relaxation and focus. Find a quiet space, sit comfortably, and listen to a guided meditation that focuses on intuition and emotional healing.
- **Breathwork Exercises**: Engage in breathwork exercises to calm the mind and reduce anxiety. Practice deep, intentional breathing to improve focus and emotional regulation. Use CBD to enhance relaxation during breathwork sessions.

Creative Expression

- **Journaling and Writing**: Keep a journal to reflect on experiences, thoughts, and ideas. Use a hemp journal and CBD to promote relaxation and clarity while writing. Reflect on personal growth, set intentions, and explore new ideas. Writing poetry, stories, or dream journals can be particularly fulfilling for Pisces.
- **Art and Music Projects**: Engage in creative projects like painting, drawing, or playing musical instruments to express emotions and ideas. Use CBD to reduce anxiety and enhance creative flow. Allow your intuition to guide your artistic process and enjoy the satisfaction of creating something meaningful.

Health and Wellness

- **Healthy Eating**: Practice mindful eating to nourish the body and mind. Choose nutritious, whole foods and savor each bite. Use CBD to promote relaxation and enhance the mindful eating experience.
- **Exercise Routine**: Incorporate regular physical exercise into the routine to promote physical health and emotional well-being. Use CBD to alleviate muscle soreness and enhance relaxation

after workouts. Activities like swimming, yoga, or dance can be particularly beneficial for Pisces.

Goal Setting and Planning

- **Task Management**: Set specific, measurable goals and track progress regularly. Use a planner or digital tool to stay organized and motivated. Incorporate CBD into the routine to maintain focus and reduce stress while working towards goals.
- **Vision Boarding**: Create a vision board to visualize goals and aspirations. Use images, quotes, and symbols that resonate with Pisces's desire for creativity and empathy. Place the vision board in a prominent location as a daily reminder of their path. Use CBD to promote relaxation and focus while creating the vision board.

Social Engagement

- **Hosting Gatherings**: Pisceans enjoy socializing and creating nurturing environments for their loved ones. Host gatherings with friends and family, incorporating CBD-infused foods and drinks. Create a relaxing and inviting atmosphere for your guests to enjoy deep conversations and connections.
- **Joining Clubs and Groups**: Engage in social clubs or interest groups that align with Pisces's passions. Use CBD to manage social anxiety and enhance positive interactions. Participate in group activities and enjoy the sense of community and connection.

Personal Development

- **Positive Affirmations**: Practice positive affirmations to reinforce confidence and emotional balance. Write down affirmations like

"I trust my intuition and follow my dreams" or "I am compassionate and connected." Repeat these affirmations daily to cultivate a positive mindset.

- **Conflict Resolution**: Develop conflict resolution skills to manage Pisces's sensitivity and idealism. Use CBD to promote calm and focus during difficult conversations. Practice active listening, empathy, and assertive communication to resolve conflicts constructively.

Self-Care and Relaxation

- **Spa Day at Home**: Create a spa day at home using CBD-infused products. Enjoy a facial mask, body scrub, and relaxing bath. Use CBD lotions and oils for self-massage. This practice can help Pisces feel pampered and rejuvenated.
- **Relaxing Bath Ritual**: Create a relaxing bath ritual using CBD-infused bath bombs or salts. Add calming essential oils like lavender or chamomile. Light candles and play soothing music to enhance the sensory experience. Soak in the warm water, letting go of stress and tension.

Learning and Exploration

- **Continual Learning**: Embrace Pisces's love for knowledge and personal growth by continually learning new skills or exploring new interests. Take classes, attend workshops, or engage in self-directed learning. Use CBD to enhance focus and reduce stress during the learning process.
- **Travel and Adventure**: Plan adventures or travel experiences that align with Pisces's love for exploration and new experiences. Use CBD to manage travel-related stress and enhance enjoyment. Reflect on the lessons and insights gained from these experiences.

Community Engagement

- **Volunteering and Service**: Engage in volunteer work or community service projects. Use CBD to manage stress and maintain emotional balance while helping others. Reflect on the sense of fulfillment and connection gained from giving back.
- **Public Speaking and Networking**: Pisces's empathetic and compassionate nature can be honed through public speaking and networking events. Use CBD to reduce anxiety and enhance confidence. Practice speeches, engage in discussions, and build connections within your community.

Emotional and Physical Health

- **Yoga and Physical Exercise**: Incorporate physical exercise, such as yoga, into the routine to promote physical health and emotional well-being. Use CBD to alleviate muscle soreness and enhance relaxation after workouts.
- **Health Checkups**: Regular health checkups and wellness routines can help Pisces stay on top of their physical health. Use CBD to reduce anxiety related to medical appointments and promote overall well-being.

In this chapter, we have explored the characteristics and traits of Pisces, the benefits of using hemp to support their intuition and empathy, and various rituals and practices to enhance their dreamy nature. By understanding the compassionate and creative nature of Pisces and incorporating hemp products into their routine, Pisces individuals can harness their strengths, balance their challenges, and achieve personal and professional growth. As we continue our journey through this book, we will discover more ways to integrate hemp and astrology for holistic healing and personal development.

Check out my Virtual dispensary for all your hemp needs: https://shift.store/sg1fan23477/retail

Chapter 37: Integrating Hemp and Astrology into Daily Life Practical Tips for Everyday Use

Integrating hemp and astrology into your daily life can enhance your well-being, promote balance, and help you connect more deeply with the rhythms of the cosmos. Here are some practical tips to seamlessly incorporate these elements into your everyday routine:

1. Morning Rituals:

- **Start with Intention:** Begin your day by setting an intention based on your zodiac sign's energy. For example, an Aries might set an intention to channel their dynamic energy into a productive task.
- **CBD-Infused Breakfast:** Incorporate CBD into your morning meal. Add CBD oil to your smoothie, coffee, or breakfast bowl to promote calm and focus.
- **Daily Horoscope Check:** Read your daily horoscope to gain insights into the energies and challenges you might face. Reflect on how these predictions align with your intentions for the day.

2. Work and Productivity:

- **Enhanced Focus:** Use CBD products like tinctures or capsules to enhance concentration and reduce anxiety. This can be especially helpful during work or study sessions.
- **Astrological Timing:** Plan important tasks or meetings according to astrological transits. For instance, Mercury retrograde might be a good time for review and reflection rather than starting new projects.

3. Self-Care Practices:

- **Meditation and Yoga:** Incorporate guided meditations or yoga sessions that align with your astrological sign. Use CBD to enhance relaxation and deepen your practice.
- **Skincare Routine:** Use CBD-infused skincare products to nourish your skin while enjoying the calming effects of hemp. Tailor your skincare routine to the current moon phase for added benefit.
- **Aromatherapy:** Use essential oils that correspond to your zodiac sign's element (fire, earth, air, water) to create a harmonious environment. Combine with CBD oil for a soothing effect.

4. Emotional and Mental Well-being:

- **Journaling:** Keep a journal to record your thoughts, dreams, and reflections. Use CBD to help clear your mind and enhance focus. Consider reflecting on how current astrological events impact your emotions.
- **Breathwork:** Engage in breathwork exercises to calm the mind and reduce stress. Incorporate CBD to enhance relaxation during these sessions.

5. Nutrition and Wellness:

- **Mindful Eating:** Practice mindful eating by incorporating CBD into your diet. Choose foods that align with your astrological sign's health needs (e.g., leafy greens for earth signs).
- **Physical Exercise:** Use CBD to alleviate muscle soreness and improve recovery after workouts. Tailor your exercise routine to the current astrological influences (e.g., high-energy workouts during a full moon).

6. Social and Relationships:

- **Hosting Gatherings:** Host gatherings with friends and family, incorporating CBD-infused foods and drinks. Create an environment that aligns with astrological themes (e.g., a Leo-themed party with bold decorations).
- **Conflict Resolution:** Use CBD to promote calm and focus during difficult conversations. Employ conflict resolution techniques that align with your astrological sign's strengths (e.g., Libra's diplomacy).

Creating a Holistic Lifestyle with Hemp and Astrology

Creating a holistic lifestyle involves integrating hemp and astrology into various aspects of your daily routine to promote overall well-being. Here are some strategies to develop a harmonious and balanced life:

1. Aligning with the Moon Phases:

- **New Moon:** Set new intentions and goals. Use CBD to enhance relaxation and clarity during meditation and intention-setting rituals.
- **Waxing Moon:** Focus on growth and progress. Incorporate energizing CBD products to maintain momentum.
- **Full Moon:** Reflect on achievements and release what no longer serves you. Use CBD for calming and grounding rituals.
- **Waning Moon:** Engage in introspection and preparation for new beginnings. Use CBD to support relaxation and deep thinking.

2. Seasonal Practices:

- **Spring Equinox:** Focus on renewal and growth. Incorporate CBD into detox routines and set new wellness goals.
- **Summer Solstice:** Embrace vitality and abundance. Use CBD to stay calm and balanced during active periods.

- **Autumn Equinox:** Reflect on gratitude and balance. Incorporate grounding CBD products into your daily routine.
- **Winter Solstice:** Embrace rest and introspection. Use CBD to support relaxation and restorative practices.

3. Tailoring to Zodiac Elements:

- **Fire Signs (Aries, Leo, Sagittarius):** Use CBD to balance high energy and promote relaxation. Engage in activities that ignite passion and creativity.
- **Earth Signs (Taurus, Virgo, Capricorn):** Incorporate CBD to enhance grounding practices and support physical health. Focus on stability and practical achievements.
- **Air Signs (Gemini, Libra, Aquarius):** Use CBD to calm the mind and enhance focus. Engage in intellectual pursuits and social connections.
- **Water Signs (Cancer, Scorpio, Pisces):** Use CBD to support emotional balance and enhance intuition. Engage in creative and spiritual practices.

Success Stories and Final Thoughts

While real-life case studies are not included, envisioning potential success stories can help illustrate the benefits of integrating hemp and astrology into daily life:

1. Improved Mental Clarity and Focus: Imagine a Virgo who struggles with perfectionism and overthinking. By incorporating CBD into their routine, they find it easier to focus on tasks without becoming overwhelmed by details. Regular meditation and journaling help them stay grounded and balanced, enhancing their productivity and well-being.

2. Enhanced Emotional Balance: Consider a Pisces who experiences emotional overwhelm due to their empathetic nature. Using CBD, they manage stress and anxiety more effectively. By aligning their self-care practices with moon phases, they experience greater emotional stability and a deeper connection to their intuition.

3. Increased Creativity and Inspiration: Picture a Leo who seeks to express their creativity through art. Incorporating CBD into their daily routine helps reduce anxiety and enhances their creative flow. By setting intentions during the new moon and reflecting during the full moon, they find themselves more inspired and productive in their artistic endeavors.

4. Improved Physical Health and Recovery: Envision a Capricorn who pushes themselves hard in their career and physical fitness. By using CBD to alleviate muscle soreness and promote relaxation, they maintain high energy levels and avoid burnout. Regular exercise and mindful eating, aligned with astrological insights, support their overall health and well-being.

Final Thoughts

Integrating hemp and astrology into your daily life offers a holistic approach to well-being that honors both your physical and spiritual needs. By understanding the unique characteristics of your astrological sign and leveraging the benefits of hemp, you can create a balanced and fulfilling lifestyle. Whether you seek to enhance your creativity, improve your focus, or find emotional balance, the combination of hemp and astrology provides powerful tools for personal growth and self-discovery. As you embark on this journey, remember to listen to your intuition, honor your unique path, and embrace the transformative power of the stars and the healing properties of hemp.

Check out my Virtual dispensary for all your hemp needs: https://shift.store/sg1fan23477/retail

Conclusion
Recap of the Healing Power of Hemp and Astrology
Throughout this book, we have explored the profound synergy between hemp and astrology, two ancient practices that offer powerful tools for holistic healing and personal development. Hemp, with its myriad benefits, provides a natural means of promoting physical, emotional, and mental well-being. Astrology, with its deep insights into the cosmic forces that shape our lives, offers a framework for understanding ourselves and our place in the universe. Together, they create a comprehensive approach to health and self-awareness that honors both our earthly existence and our connection to the cosmos.

The Healing Power of Hemp:

- **Physical Wellness:** Hemp, particularly products containing CBD, has been shown to alleviate pain, reduce inflammation, and promote relaxation. By incorporating hemp into your daily routine, you can support your body's natural healing processes and maintain physical health.
- **Emotional Balance:** Hemp's anxiolytic properties help reduce stress and anxiety, promoting emotional stability and resilience. Regular use of CBD can enhance your ability to manage life's challenges and maintain a positive outlook.
- **Mental Clarity:** Hemp supports mental clarity and focus, helping you stay sharp and engaged. Whether you are working, studying, or pursuing creative endeavors, CBD can enhance your cognitive abilities and improve your performance.

The Wisdom of Astrology:

- **Self-Awareness:** Astrology provides a deep understanding of your unique personality, strengths, and challenges. By studying your astrological chart, you can gain valuable insights into your inner nature and navigate your life with greater self-awareness.
- **Timing and Alignment:** Astrology helps you align your actions with the cosmic rhythms, enhancing your ability to make the most of opportunities and avoid pitfalls. By timing important decisions and activities according to astrological transits, you can optimize your success and well-being.
- **Spiritual Connection:** Astrology connects you to the larger universe, fostering a sense of belonging and purpose. By understanding your place in the cosmic order, you can cultivate a deeper sense of meaning and fulfillment in your life.

Encouragement for Continued Exploration and Integration

As you continue your journey with hemp and astrology, remember that these practices are not static but dynamic and evolving. Each day brings new opportunities to deepen your understanding and refine your approach. Here are some ways to continue your exploration and integration:

1. Stay Curious: Keep learning about hemp and astrology. Explore new products, techniques, and astrological insights. Read books, attend workshops, and engage with communities that share your interests.

2. Experiment and Adapt: Tailor your use of hemp and astrology to your unique needs and preferences. Experiment with different CBD products and dosages to find what works best for you. Adjust your astrological practices based on your experiences and insights.

3. Reflect and Adjust: Regularly reflect on your experiences with hemp and astrology. Consider keeping a journal to track your progress, note your observations, and refine your practices. Use these reflections to make informed adjustments and continue growing.

4. Share and Connect: Share your knowledge and experiences with others. Engage in discussions, join online forums, and connect with like-minded individuals. By sharing and learning from others, you can enrich your own journey and contribute to a broader community of wellness and self-discovery.

Final Reflections and Future Directions

As we conclude this book, it is important to reflect on the transformative potential of integrating hemp and astrology into your life. By embracing these ancient practices, you are taking a proactive approach to your well-being, honoring both your physical needs and your spiritual aspirations.

Embrace the Journey: Remember that the path to holistic healing and self-awareness is a journey, not a destination. Be patient with yourself, celebrate your progress, and embrace the ongoing process of growth and discovery.

Future Directions: The fields of hemp and astrology are continually evolving, offering new insights and opportunities. Stay open to emerging research, new products, and innovative techniques. By staying informed and adaptable, you can continue to benefit from the latest advancements and deepen your practice.

Holistic Integration: Ultimately, the goal of integrating hemp and astrology is to create a balanced and fulfilling life. By combining the healing properties of hemp with the wisdom of astrology, you can navigate your life with greater ease, purpose, and joy. Embrace this holistic approach, and let it guide you toward a healthier, more harmonious existence.

As you move forward, may you find inspiration in the stars and healing in the earth, and may your journey with hemp and astrology bring you profound peace, joy, and self-awareness. Thank you for embarking on this journey, and may it continue to enrich your life in countless ways.

Appendix
Glossary of Terms
Astrology Terms:

- **Ascendant (Rising Sign):** The zodiac sign that was rising on the eastern horizon at the time of your birth, influencing your outward behavior and appearance.
- **Aspect:** The angular relationship between two planets in a birth chart, indicating how they interact and influence each other.
- **Cardinal Signs:** Aries, Cancer, Libra, and Capricorn; known for initiating action and leading change.
- **Celestial Events:** Significant occurrences in the sky, such as eclipses, meteor showers, and solstices.
- **Conjunction:** An aspect where two planets are close together, combining their energies.
- **Cusp:** The dividing line between two zodiac signs or houses.
- **Descendant:** The zodiac sign opposite the Ascendant, representing partnerships and relationships.
- **Elements:** Fire, Earth, Air, and Water; each zodiac sign is associated with one element that influences its traits.
- **Fixed Signs:** Taurus, Leo, Scorpio, and Aquarius; known for stability and determination.
- **Houses:** Twelve divisions of the birth chart, each representing different areas of life.
- **Mutable Signs:** Gemini, Virgo, Sagittarius, and Pisces; known for adaptability and flexibility.
- **Natal Chart (Birth Chart):** A map of the sky at the time of your birth, showing the positions of the planets and their influence on your personality.
- **Retrograde:** The apparent backward motion of a planet, often associated with reflection and revisiting past issues.

- **Transit:** The current movement of planets in relation to their positions in your natal chart.

Hemp Terms:

- **CBD (Cannabidiol):** A non-psychoactive compound found in hemp that has various therapeutic benefits.
- **Endocannabinoid System (ECS):** A biological system in the body that interacts with cannabinoids and helps regulate various physiological processes.
- **Full-Spectrum CBD:** CBD extract that contains all cannabinoids, terpenes, and other beneficial compounds found in the hemp plant.
- **Hemp:** A variety of the Cannabis sativa plant species grown specifically for industrial use and low in THC.
- **Isolate:** Pure CBD without any other cannabinoids, terpenes, or plant compounds.
- **Terpenes:** Aromatic compounds found in hemp and other plants that contribute to their scent and therapeutic effects.
- **THC (Tetrahydrocannabinol):** The psychoactive compound in cannabis that produces a "high"; present in very low amounts in hemp.

Recommended Resources
Books:

- *Astrology for the Soul* by Jan Spiller: An in-depth exploration of the influence of the North Node in your birth chart.
- *The Only Astrology Book You'll Ever Need* by Joanna Martine Woolfolk: A comprehensive guide to astrology and its various aspects.

- *Medical Marijuana & CBD: A Beginner's Guide* by Dr. Rachna Patel: An accessible introduction to the therapeutic uses of CBD and medical marijuana.
- *The Art and Science of Hand Reading* by Ellen Goldberg and Dorian Bergen: A detailed guide to palmistry and understanding the lines and shapes of the hands.

Websites:

- **Astro.com:** Offers free birth charts, horoscopes, and extensive articles on astrology.
- **Cafe Astrology:** Provides detailed astrological reports, daily horoscopes, and educational resources.
- **Project CBD:** A comprehensive resource for information on CBD, its uses, and research.
- **Leafly:** A website that offers information on different strains of cannabis, including hemp, and their effects.

Products:

- **Charlotte's Web:** A well-known brand offering high-quality CBD oils, capsules, and gummies.
- **NuLeaf Naturals:** Offers full-spectrum CBD oil made from organic hemp.
- **Endoca:** Provides a variety of CBD products, including oils, capsules, and skincare items.
- **Koi CBD:** Known for their high-quality CBD vape juices, tinctures, and topical products.

Detailed Charts and Tables

Moon Phases:

Phase	Description	Effects	Best Practices
New Moon	The moon is not visible.	Beginnings, setting intentions, renewal	Meditation, goal setting, planning
Waxing Crescent	A small sliver of the moon is visible.	Growth, creativity, action	Start new projects, take small steps
First Quarter	Half of the moon is visible.	Challenges, decision making, strength	Face obstacles, make decisions, persevere
Waxing Gibbous	More than half of the moon is visible.	Refinement, progress, momentum	Fine-tune plans, stay focused, keep going
Full Moon	The entire moon is visible.	Culmination, illumination, release	Reflect, celebrate achievements, let go
Waning Gibbous	The moon starts to decrease in size.	Gratitude, sharing, introspection	Express gratitude, share knowledge, reflect
Last Quarter	Half of the moon is visible.	Release, forgiveness, transition	Let go of what no longer serves, forgive
Waning Crescent	A small sliver of the moon is visible.	Rest, surrender, preparation	Rest, recharge, prepare for new beginnings

Celestial Events:

Event	Date Range	Description	Effects
Spring Equinox	Around March 20	Day and night are equal; marks the beginning of spring.	Renewal, growth, new beginnings
Summer Solstice	Around June 21	Longest day of the year; marks the beginning of summer.	Vitality, abundance, energy
Autumn Equinox	Around September 22	Day and night are equal; marks the beginning of autumn.	Balance, reflection, harvest
Winter Solstice	Around December 21	Shortest day of the year; marks the beginning of winter.	Introspection, rest, renewal
Solar Eclipses	Varies (2-5 times per year)	The moon blocks the sun, casting a shadow on Earth.	Transformation, new insights, change
Lunar Eclipses	Varies (2-5 times per year)	The Earth casts a shadow on the moon.	Emotional release, closure, revelation
Meteor Showers	Varies (e.g., Perseids in August)	Earth passes through debris left by comets.	Inspiration, awe, heightened energy

Planetary Alignments:

Alignment	Description	Effects
Conjunction	Two planets are close together in the sky.	Intense energy, focus, new beginnings
Opposition	Two planets are opposite each other in the sky.	Tension, balance, awareness
Square	Two planets are 90 degrees apart.	Challenge, action, growth
Trine	Two planets are 120 degrees apart.	Harmony, ease, opportunity
Sextile	Two planets are 60 degrees apart.	Cooperation, support, potential

Frequently Asked Questions (FAQs)

Q: What is the best way to start integrating hemp and astrology into my daily life? A: Begin by incorporating small practices into your routine, such as reading your daily horoscope and using CBD products like oils or edibles. Gradually expand your practices to include meditation, intention-setting, and aligning your activities with moon phases and astrological transits.

Q: How do I choose the right CBD product for my needs? A: Consider your specific needs and preferences. For general wellness, CBD oil or capsules are a good start. For targeted relief, try CBD topicals like balms or creams. Ensure you choose high-quality products from reputable brands that provide third-party lab testing results.

Q: How can I use astrology to improve my relationships? A: Understanding your own astrological chart and your partner's can provide insights into your compatibility and communication styles. Use this knowledge to enhance empathy, resolve conflicts, and strengthen your connection. Aligning your activities with favorable astrological transits can also improve harmony in relationships.

Q: What are the benefits of aligning my activities with moon phases? A: Aligning your activities with moon phases can help you harness the natural rhythms of growth, reflection, and release. For example, setting intentions during the new moon can enhance your focus on new goals, while reflecting and releasing during the full moon can help you let go of what no longer serves you.

Q: Can I use hemp and astrology together for personal growth? A: Yes, combining hemp and astrology can enhance your personal growth journey. Use CBD to support relaxation and focus during astrological practices like meditation, intention-setting, and journaling. This combination can help you gain deeper insights, reduce stress, and promote overall well-being.

Q: How can I stay updated on new developments in hemp and astrology? A: Follow reputable websites, subscribe to newsletters, and join online communities dedicated to hemp and astrology. Reading books, attending workshops, and participating in webinars can also help you stay informed about the latest research and trends in these fields.

This appendix provides a comprehensive guide to integrating hemp and astrology into your daily life. By exploring the glossary of terms, recommended resources, detailed charts, and frequently asked questions, you can deepen your understanding and enhance your practice. Embrace the healing power of hemp and the wisdom of astrology to create a balanced, fulfilling, and harmonious lifestyle.

<u>Message from the Author:</u>

I hope you enjoyed this book, I love astrology and knew there was not a book such as this out on the shelf. I love metaphysical items as well. Please check out my other books:

-Life of Government Benefits

-My life of Hell

-My life with Hydrocephalus

-Red Sky

-World Domination:Woman's rule

-World Domination:Woman's Rule 2: The War

-Life and Banishment of Apophis: book 1

-The Kidney Friendly Diet

-The Ultimate Hemp Cookbook

-Creating a Dispensary(legally)

-Cleanliness throughout life: the importance of showering from childhood to adulthood.

-Strong Roots: The Risks of Overcoddling children

-Hemp Horoscopes: Cosmic Insights and Earthly Healing

- Celestial Hemp Navigating the Zodiac: Through the Green Cosmos

-Astrological Hemp: Aligning The Stars with Earth's Ancient Herb

-The Astrological Guide to Hemp: Stars, Signs, and Sacred Leaves

-Green Growth: Innovative Marketing Strategies for your Hemp Products and Dispensary

-Cosmic Cannabis

-Astrological Munchies

-Henry The Hemp

-Zodiacal Roots: The Astrological Soul Of Hemp

- Green Constellations: Intersection of Hemp and Zodiac

-Hemp in The Houses: An astrological Adventure Through The Cannabis Galaxy

-Galactic Ganja Guide

Heavenly Hemp

Zodiac Leaves

Doctor Who Astrology

Cannastrology

Stellar Satvias and Cosmic Indicas

Celestial Cannabis: A Zodiac Journey

AstroHerbology: The Sky and The Soil: Volume 1

AstroHerbology:Celestial Cannabis:Volume 2

Cosmic Cannabis Cultivation

The Starry Guide to Herbal Harmony: Volume 1

The Starry Guide to Herbal Harmony: Cannabis Universe: Volume 2

Yugioh Astrology: Astrological Guide to Deck, Duels and more

Nightmare Mansion: Echoes of The Abyss

Nightmare Mansion 2: Legacy of Shadows

Nightmare Mansion 3: Shadows of the Forgotten

Nightmare Mansion 4: Echoes of the Damned

The Life and Banishment of Apophis: Book 2

Nightmare Mansion: Halls of Despair

Healing with Herb: Cannabis and Hydrocephalus

Planetary Pot: Aligning with Astrological Herbs: Volume 1

Fast Track to Freedom: 30 Days to Financial Independence Using AI, Assets, and Agile Hustles

Cosmic Hemp Pathways

How to Become Financially Free in 30 Days: 10,000 Paths to Prosperity

Zodiacal Herbage: Astrological Insights: Volume 1

Nightmare Mansion: Whispers in the Walls

The Daleks Invade Atlantis

Henry the hemp and Hydrocephalus

10X The Kidney Friendly Diet
  Cannabis Universe: Adult coloring book

10X The Kidney Friendly Diet

Check out my Virtual dispensary for all your hemp needs: https://shift.store/sg1fan23477/retail

If you want solar for your home go here: https://www.harborsolar.live/apophisenterprises/

Get some shirts: https://www.bonfire.com/store/apophis-shirt-emporium/

Instagrams:

@apophis_enterprises,

@hempkingdom2024,

@apophisbookemporium,

@apophisfashion,

@apophisscardshop

Twitter: @apophisenterpr1, Tiktok:@apophisenterprise

Youtube: @sg1fan23477

Podcast:Apophis Chat Zone: https://open.spotify.com/show/5zXbrCLEV2xzCp8ybrfHsk?si=fb4d4fdbdce44dec

Newsletter: https://apophiss-newsletter-27c897.beehiiv.com/

www.ingramcontent.com/pod-product-compliance
Lightning Source LLC
Chambersburg PA
CBHW051817150726
47998CB00001B/188